FOLK HARPS

Celtic harp made by
Mr. Edward C. Penduck
Elsternwick, Victoria, Australia

FOLK HARPS

GILDAS JAFFRENNOU

Model and Allied Publications Limited
Book Division, Station Road, Kings Langley, Herts.

ACKNOWLEDGEMENTS

The author is grateful to the following for assistance and information:
The Royal Marine School of Music, Deal, Kent.
Wilfred Smith, harp maker, 15 Castelnau, Barnes, London, SW13.
Dennis Miller, Lledrod, Llansilin, Oswestry, Salop.
The South American Missionary Society, 157 Waterloo Road, London, SE1.
L. Gathier & Co. Ltd., 6 Charterhouse Square, London, EC1.
Archdeacon A. J. Barratt, Santiago 1862, San Miguel de Tucuman, Argentina.
Mrs. Graciela Scorza de Jauregui, Embajada del Paraguay, London.
R. Buisson, Ingénieur en chef du Génie Rural, Lyon (France).

Model and Allied Publications Limited
Book Division, Station Road, Kings Langley, Herts.

First Published 1973
© Gildas Jaffrennou 1973
ISBN 0 852 42313 6

Phototypeset by Filmtype
Services Limited, Scarborough
Printed and Bound in England by
G. A. Pindar & Son Ltd, Scarborough

CONTENTS

INTRODUCTION

Harps are among the
oldest musical instruments
and were probably
suggested by the stretched
string of the bow which
produces a musical sound
when it is struck by the
finger. There are records
of harps being played as
far back as 3000 BC in
Mesopotamia and Egypt
and they were also popular
in Greece and Rome.
Indeed, they appear always
to have existed in all
places inhabited by men or
spirits, except in Hell . . !

The true origin of the Western European harp is
very difficult to trace. Perhaps it was invented by
those skilful woodworkers, the Vikings, or by the
Irish, the Welsh or the Dutch—nobody knows. The
earliest drawings of harps appear in the Utrecht
Psalter, a Carolingian manuscript written circa
816 AD. Some of the harps depicted in the
illuminated drawings resemble Celtic harps, others
resemble the type we call "Minstrel", and others
are like the harps of ancient Egypt. In Ireland,
however, there are relief carvings of harps on stone
crosses dating from about the same period as the
Dutch manuscripts.

A historian of music, Vincentio Galilei, in a
work printed in Florence in 1581, is quoted as
saying: ". . . this most ancient instrument was
brought to us from Ireland, where they are
excellently made and in great numbers; the
inhabitants of that island having practised on it
for many, many ages . . ." The mediaeval harp of
O'Brian, at Trinity College, Dublin, has 30 strings
and is 72 centimetres high. The sound-box is made

6

of red willow, the curved pillar of oak, and the neck is covered with embossed silver. The harps which were used in Wales and Scotland during the Middle Ages were almost identical to the Irish ones, and so was the "Cithara Anglica". These harps were played by early Christian missionaries, but they soon became the traditional instruments of the bards, minstrels, trouvères, and troubadours. Gradually, they were adopted by the lords of the land, and so became a symbol of wealth and power.

In 920, it was considered that three things were essential to a gentleman: a harp, a cloak, and a chess-board. Three conditions also were necessary for his happiness: a faithful wife, a well-padded chair, and *a harp well tuned*. When Richard I (Coeur de Lion) escaped from Austria, he gave Blondel de Nesle the title of "First Harper of England" in acknowledgement of his services during the escape. Harpers then had special privileges, and were considered to be among the highest intellectuals of the time. The instrument itself was treated with great respect, and every noble household in the country possessed its hereditary harp, handed down through the generations for the use of the lord or his domestic bard and teacher.

The word "harp" is of Teutonic origin, but the Celts had two different names for it. In Ireland, Scotland, and the Isle of Man, it was and is still called "clarsach". In Wales, Cornwall, and Brittany it is called "telyn". This could support the theory that harps were known to the Celts before the word "harp" was introduced by invaders from the Continent. However, by the 13th century, harps very similar to the Celtic type were in common use all over Europe. These mediaeval instruments were *modal*, that is to say, they could not play accidentals.

The strings were tuned in the Dorian scale (Ray mode): D, E, F, G, A, B, C, D, without sharps or flats, or in such gapped scales as were in use at the time. It is interesting to notice that the "HWYL" chanting of Welsh preachers is derived from that mode, and so is the recitative chanting of Breton popular poetry. Mr. A. Dolmetsch has demonstrated that the ancient Welsh music of Robert ap Huw was composed on a Celtic harp tuned in the Ray mode. The old harp had obvious limitations and it was superseded by better instruments such as the lute and the crwth until an unknown harpist, presumably from Wales, invented a harp with two rows of strings capable of producing sharps and flats. From Wales, this new harp spread to Italy in the 15th century, and it became known there as "arpia doppia" or double harp. The Germans adopted the Italian harp and called it "doppel harpf".

At the end of the 17th century, another Welshman improved the double harp still further, and it became a treble or triple harp with three rows of strings. The outer strings were tuned diatonically, and the inner rows had the sharps and flats. There still exist a few harpists in Wales who can play the treble harp, in particular a very distinguished harpist from Dolgelley, Telenores Ardudwy. The instrument is capable of most amazing effects, but is very difficult to play.

At about the same time as the Welshman invented the treble harp, an Austrian made a big improvement to the mediaeval harp. He put hooks on some strings, whereby they could be shortened by one semitone; later on all strings were provided with hooks. The traditional harps of Ireland, Scotland, and the Tyrol are of this type. Some years before the invention of the harp with semitones, Christian missionaries introduced the harp to South America and there it has remained a harp without sharps or flats. The harp makers of Paraguay and Argentina improved the structure of the harp itself by securing the strings in the centre of the neck instead of attaching them to the side of the neck. These harps are classified as "perpendicular". Most other harps have the pillar slightly out of the vertical. The peculiar design of the Paraguayan harp accounts for its brilliant tone; it is known as "Arpa India", and is now the traditional instrument of the Guarani Indians, made famous all over the world by such extraordinary performers as Félix Perez Cardozo, Santiago Cortezi, Digno Garcia, Roberto Guarani, and the famous group "Los Paraguayos".

Under the sponsorship of an Englishman (Archdeacon Barratt of the South American Missionary Society), a group of young harpists called "Los Picaflores" (The Humming Birds) has been responsible for introducing the Paraguayan harp to the British public in the TV programme "Stars on Sunday". These talented harpists are the children of Archdeacon Barratt, Terry, Rosemary, Hilary and Patricia, and their harps were made in Asuncio by Eladio Rojas. Another famous harp maker who should be mentioned is Christino Baez from Asuncio Monges.

Modern Paraguayan harps are provided with guitar mechanisms which make them easy to tune. Folk harps are being revived all over the world because they are good musical instruments in their own right. There is now a revival of the Celtic harp in Brittany, with well over one hundred good players in the country, and several harp makers such as Jord Cochevelou, Claude and Michel Leroux, and Daniel Paris. The best known Breton harpist is a young man called Alan Stivel who has given recitals in many countries and made many records. Folk harps are easy to learn and easy to play; they are ideal as an introduction to the concert harp, and they have an enormous advantage over the latter—they are portable. The skilled woodworker and craftsman will find tremendous satisfaction in making his own harp, and if the reader follows my instructions, he should not go wrong. So, let us to work.

CHAPTER 1

THREE METHODS FOR MAKING THE SOUNDBOX OR 'BODY'

The main purpose of this book is to serve as a manual for the amateur harp maker but it only deals with Folk harps, which are not difficult to make. Three types of Folk harps are described: the Celtic harp, the Minstrel harp and the harp of Paraguay also called "Arpa India".

The Celtic and Minstrel harps have the same body, and the same number of strings. The body is usually made of wood, but it can also be made of glass fibre and wood. When glass fibre is used, the harp is capable of withstanding greater stress without impairing the quality of sound in any way. We shall endeavour to describe three methods of construction, and the reader can choose the one that suits him best.

METHODS OF CONSTRUCTION No. 1

The following timber is required.

No. req'd	Description	Long	Wide	Thick	Material
12	Strips for skin	1100	50	6	Parana pine or agba
1	Back	1100	18	10	Parana pine, agba
1	Frames	700	40	10	Plywood
1	Base	500	500	20	Blockboard
3	Sheets of veneer	1100	300		Mahogany, sapele
1	Strip	1100	40		Formica sheet

All measurements are given in millimetres.

The first thing to do is to cut out the frames as shown in Fig. 1.1. For frame A you can take a piece out of the blockboard for the base and glue a piece of ordinary three-ply on top in order to obtain the required thickness of 25mm. From the dimensions on Fig. 1.1, draw the full size pattern on stiff paper or card. You need two tracings for this; one for the outside pattern and one for the inside. Transfer the drawings to your piece of wood and shape it accordingly. The little recess for the under string bar can be made at a later stage.

Frame E: This is the bottom part of the harp, and it is at an angle of 58 degrees with the sound-board. First, draw on paper or card a series of parallel lines 24mm apart, (a sheet of paper 450mm by 450mm is required). In the centre, draw the axis line and on each side of it mark the offsets taken from drawing E, Fig. 1.1. Join all points by a sweet curve. Now take a piece of blockboard and by means of carbon paper, trace your drawing on to

Fig. 1.1

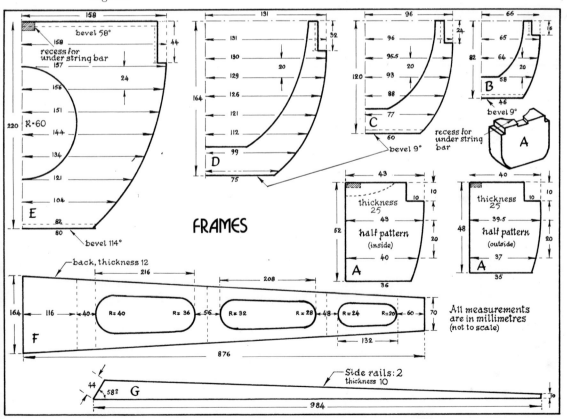

FRAMES

All measurements are in millimetres (not to scale)

13

it. Then cut along the outline with a bowsaw, or better still, a bandsaw. Cut out the circular hole in the centre of frame E with a jigsaw or bowsaw. Now, with a spokeshave, plane the angles at top and bottom only. The bevelled sides of frame E can be made later.

Frame D: Trace ten parallel lines 20mm apart on a piece of paper, draw the axis and mark the outline as you have done for frame E. Now, draw the inside curve freehand so that it is shaped like Fig. 1.1. Give it a pleasing appearance; it does not need to be exactly as on the plan and as long as the two sides are identical it will be all right. Next, take a piece of plywood 10mm thick, and transfer the pattern to the wood as before. Cut along the outline.

Frame C and Frame B are made in exactly the same manner as frame D. The next step is to make the back piece F, Fig. 1.1. Trace and cut out according to F, Fig. 1.1. The two side rails G, which have been omitted on the timber list on purpose, can be made from any good piece of fir or pine left over from a previous job. Trace and cut according to G, Fig. 1.1.

The shaped pieces of wood for the framework are now ready for assembly, so we can proceed in the following manner.

Take a stiff sheet of plywood or blockboard (1040mm by 400mm), which will serve as a temporary support for the construction. At one end, with a set square, trace a pencil line 27mm from the edge, then another line 232mm from the first one, followed by two more lines 280mm and 258mm apart, as shown on Fig. 1.2. These lines represent the sides of the frames facing the wider end of the body.

Secure frames A, B, C, and D to the temporary support by means of blocks of wood or short rails and make sure all frames are perpendicular to the base. When the setting is correct, place back piece F on top of the frames, making sure that it fits exactly. A small bevel is required on each frame, and this can easily be done with a spokeshave. Bevel the two sides of back piece F, so that they follow the curves of the frames. Now, screw back piece F in position (no glue yet), and bevel the base end.

The next step is to position side rails G in the notches. These notches, too, will require a small bevel so that the rails fit snugly in position. Do this with a file, taking great care not to upset the whole structure, which will still be weak. Alternatively, you could dismantle the whole structure when the

Fig. 1.2

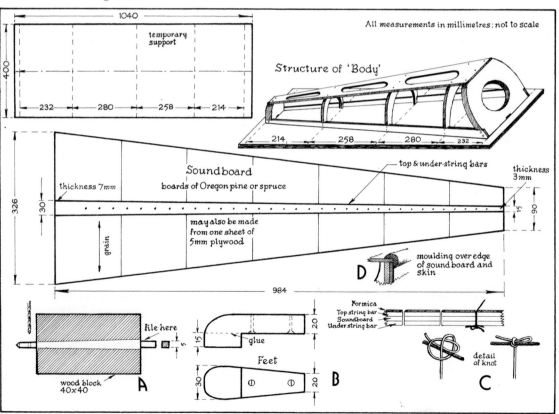

bevels have been marked, and secure the frames in the vice for filing the bevels. When the fitting is good, glue and nail side rails G in the notches, and glue and screw back piece F. All glueing is best done with resin glue.

The skin: The term "the skin" applies to the rounded back part of the body. It is made like the carvel planking of a boat.

First, divide both sides of frame E into eight sections, and do the same to frame A at the small end of the body, and this will give you the width of the 16 tapered laths used for making the skin of the harp. Cut out your laths a little bit wider in order to account for the bevels; start the "planking" at the bottom, that is to say, over rails G. Coat the rails with glue, and nail the laths in position with panel pins, one panel pin every 30mm. Be careful about the small ends of the laths: don't split them when driving the nails in!

All laths are glued on the edges, and nailed and glued to the frames. When the glue is dry, the skin can be smoothed with a disc sander first, then by hand. If you find it difficult to obtain a good joint between the wide ends of the laths and frame E, flatten the section on frame E with a file before glueing. Make sure the skin surface is nice and smooth all over because it will be covered with veneer later, and a good surface is essential for the veneer to adhere evenly to its base.

The soundboard: In musical terms, this part of the harp is also called the "table". When the harpist strikes the strings near the "table" it gives a special quality to the sound. The soundboard is flat: that is to say, it is made flat, but because of the sustained stress caused by the tension of the strings (about 1500 lb) it acquires a certain curvature, and the quality of sound improves in the process.

The soundboard is made of resinous wood such as pine or spruce, and the grain of the wood is across the table, while the thickness is gradually less towards the top of the harp. It should be about 7mm thick at the base and about 3mm thick at the top.

To make it you require two pieces of spruce, or Oregon pine of the best quality, 1000mm long, 180mm wide and 8mm thick. Cut the wood into short lengths to cover the surface of the triangular table, leaving about 40mm excess on each side; in other words, make a broader triangle than is actually required. Now, you could plane some wood off the thickness of each short plank until you gradually reach the thickness of 3mm for the shorter piece, but it is not a very satisfactory process. It is much better to make a jig as described in Fig. 1.3.

When this is made, cover the top part with newspaper, screw the two temporary battens from underneath (no glue), place the longest piece of timber over the jig and battens, mark holes for two screws each side and make pilot holes for the screws. Each short plank will be screwed and glued to the battens. Put glue also on the butt joint between each plank. The newspaper will prevent the soundboard from adhering to the jig. When the glue is dry, remove the screws from the top so that the whole surface can now be planed, scraped, and glasspapered. To do this you must, of course,

Fig. 1.3

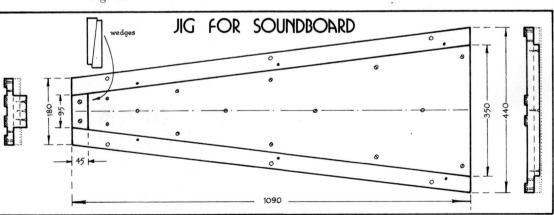

secure the jig to the bench by means of four screws, one at each corner.

When you are satisfied that the surface is true and smooth, draw a pencil line in the centre from top to bottom. You can now make the under string bar and also the upper string bar according to the measurements in Fig. 1.2; make sure these bars are perfectly straight. Take one bar and glue it over the pencil line on soundboard, but do not use nails. Place weights on top of the bar, and leave it overnight.

Next, unscrew the jig from the bench and release the temporary battens from the jig, handling the soundboard with care. Turn the jig over and underneath there will be a recess where the under string bar will fit snugly while you remove excess glue, and glasspaper the upper side of the soundboard.

Do this with great care. A good tip is to wet the surface with a damp cloth after you have used the finest grade of glasspaper, as the water causes the wood fibres to swell, and when the wood is dry again continue the glasspapering until the surface is beautifully smooth. Before you glue the upper string bar it must receive its Formica facing, and all the holes for the strings must be drilled; the Formica strip is glued to the upper string bar with contact adhesive.

It is difficult to mark the positions of the holes on the Formica and the best way to go about it is to apply a strip of white masking tape over the Formica and make the pencil marks on it. Having done so, put it aside because it is at this stage that you must decide what type of harp you are going to make—whether it will be Celtic, Minstrel, Paraguayan or Bardic.

So, let us consider the four types.

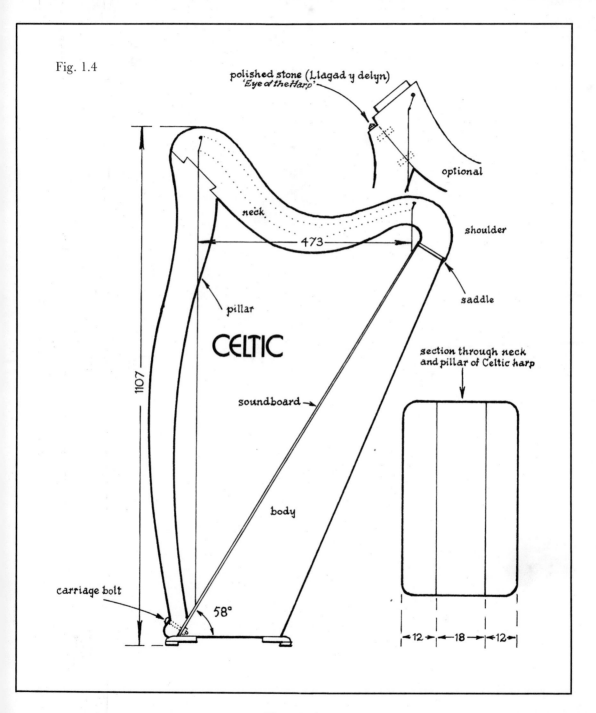

Fig. 1.4

polished stone (Llagad y delyn)
'Eye of the Harp'

optional

shoulder

neck

473

saddle

pillar

CELTIC

section through neck
and pillar of Celtic harp

soundboard

1107

body

carriage bolt

58°

|← 12 →|← 18 →|← 12 →|

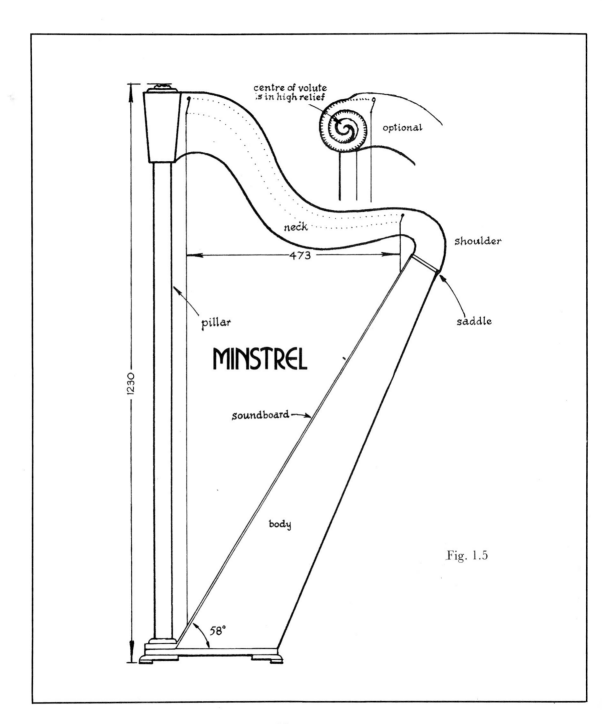

centre of volute
is in high relief

optional

neck

shoulder

saddle

473

pillar

MINSTREL

1230

soundboard

body

Fig. 1.5

58°

20

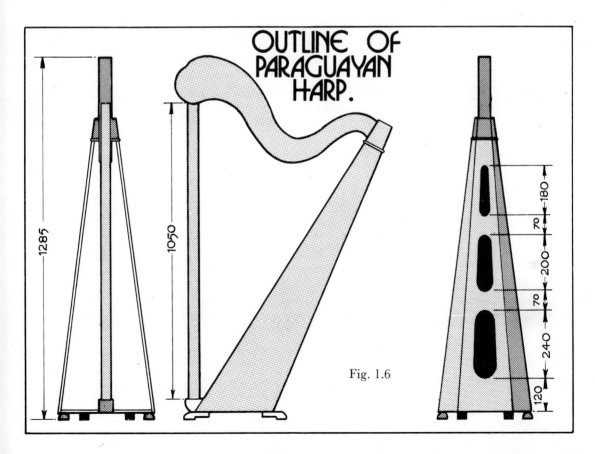

OUTLINE OF PARAGUAYAN HARP.

Fig. 1.6

21

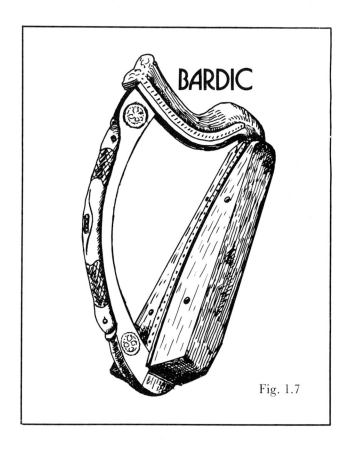

BARDIC

Fig. 1.7

As we have already seen, three have the same body and the same number of strings. See Chapter 6 for the Bardic Harp which differs in construction. The Minstrel harp and the Paraguayan harp are taller than the Celtic harp, but the latter will fit easily inside the boot of a motor-car. The others will have to be carried in the car itself with some protection in order to avoid damaging the fabric of the back seat.

The Celtic harp is the easiest to make. The neck and curved pillar present no problem of assembly; one is almost the continuation of the other. The straight pillars of the Minstrel and Paraguayan harps call for a certain amount of ornamentation, such as fluting, spiralling, or turning.

On the Minstrel harp, a capital or a volute is required at the top of the pillar, and an extra base and base plate are also needed. The Minstrel harp is in appearance like a small concert harp without the pedals, so we would expect it to be gilded and more adorned than the others.

The design of each harp must remind us of the country where it originated, whether it be the rich extravagant châteaux of France, the monasteries of Ireland with their illuminated manuscripts, or the austere but warm Paraguay. Visual appeal plays an important part in the enjoyment of harp music, and in the eighteenth century, young ladies of the aristocracy found in harp playing a charming excuse to display pretty arms or well turned ankles! A French writer of that period says that one of his friends lost his heart to a lady who was neither young nor beautiful, but whose harp playing was absolute perfection . . .!

It is a fact that people who listen to harp music keep looking at the player, and it can have an almost hypnotic effect on the audience. I will never forget a solo performance given by Miss H. Russell-Ferguson, a talented Celtic harpist, in Brittany in 1934. She almost brought the roof down, and the crowd went mad with excitement. People were crying with joy and every piece got a standing ovation. Miss Russell-Ferguson, a cool professional Scottish harpist and Folk singer, was absolutely bewildered by the reception! The harp is the only musical instrument still surrounded by a kind of magical halo.

After that digression, we must leave the workshop for the study. Take a large piece of drawing paper to make a full size drawing of your harp; a drawing in profile will suffice. First trace the soundboard and the upper string bar at an angle of 58° from the horizontal. The best way to do this is to fix the drawing paper on a wall by means of Sellotape or masking tape. Now enlarge the pattern for the neck to full size on a piece of fairly stiff drawing paper. Cut along the outline with a pair of scissors and you have a template. At the top of the soundboard line on the wall, draw a line representing the outer surface of frame A, which should be almost perpendicular to the soundboard. Next place your template in position and draw a pencil line along the edge: do not forget the height of the pillar in relation to the base.

For the Minstrel and Paraguayan harps, there is no need to make a template for the pillar because it is straight, but it is essential to make a template for the curved pillar of the Celtic harp, and to attach it with Sellotape to the neck so it becomes the downward continuation of the latter. The base of the pillar of the Minstrel harp does not rest on the soundboard, but in the case of the Celtic harp and Paraguayan harp the pillars rest on the soundboard which gives a better triangulation.

When you have made a complete full size drawing of your harp in profile, mark the position of the lowest string (No. 34) on the upper string bar. On the Celtic harp, it should be at about 100mm from the lower end of the soundboard, and the same for the Paraguayan harp. But for the Minstrel harp, 80mm will suffice. Now mark the position of the bridge-pin of string No. 34 on the neck as indicated on the plan. Draw a straight line joining that mark to the mark already made on the upper string bar; this line will then represent the lowest string of the harp, string No. 34. All other strings must be exactly parallel to this one. Here, it is well to take note that the distances between the strings are not all the same, and there are two reasons for this.

First, the vibration amplitude of bass strings is larger than it is for treble strings, therefore more space is needed between bass strings otherwise they may touch and make an ugly noise. The second reason has to do with the ease of fingering. So, the distance between string No. 34 and string No. 33 will be 18mm, but the distance between string No. 1 and string No. 2 will only be 12mm. The decreasing must be gradual and it varies from one maker to another.

I suggest the following arrangement:

From string	No. 34	to string	No. 33	=	18mm
,,	,,	No. 33	,,	No. 30	=	17mm
,,	,,	No. 30	,,	No. 24	=	16mm
,,	,,	No. 24	,,	No. 19	=	15mm
,,	,,	No. 19	,,	No. 15	=	14mm
,,	,,	No. 15	,,	No. 7	=	13mm
,,	,,	No. 7	,,	No. 1	=	12mm

Now, trace a curved line for the bridge-pins and then another one nearer the upper edge of the neck where the holes for the tuning pegs will be drilled. In order to place the tuning pegs in the right place and to avoid too great a stress on the bridge pins, the angle made by the string going over the left of the bridge pin, and then to the right of the tuning peg and around it, must not be too acute. To mark the holes for the tuning pegs, simply prolong the string lines until they meet the curved lines for the pegs; 4mm to the right, on the curved line, is correct.

When all the marking is done on the neck, fetch the upper string bar from the workshop and mark the holes for the strings as they appear on the full size drawing. Make sure they are in a straight line and in the centre of the Formica strip, and then start the drilling. It can be done by hand but if you own an electric drill on a stand, the job will be more accurate. As for the bits, you need a 3mm ($\frac{1}{8}$ in.) for hole No. 34 and up to hole No. 24. From Nos. 24 to 14, a 2mm bit will do. For the rest of the holes, use a 1.5mm bit. A very shallow chamfer must now be made in the Formica around each hole, just enough to smooth the sharp edge. If you make it too deep you may reach the underside of the Formica, and the sharp bevel will eventually cut through the strings.

You can now glue the upper string bar in position. Place weights on it and leave it overnight.

Cut the soundboard along the temporary battens, and glue it on the body of the harp, securing it to the side rails with panel pins. When the glue is dry, trim the edges.

The body of your harp is now ready for veneering and mahogany veneer is the most suitable. The whole body should be veneered including the back, but not the soundboard, of course. Pay particular attention to the three elongated holes on the back, as the veneer around these holes should be trimmed with great care in order not to split the edges. A plastic moulding should be glued around them as it will hide the edges of the veneer and enhance the appearance.

Fig. 1.8

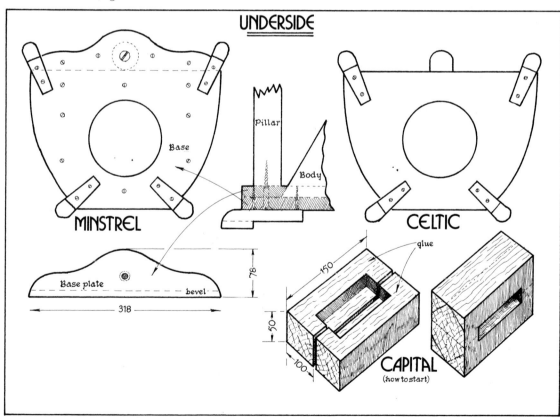

Now, another moulding, in wood or in plastic (gold), should hide the edges of the soundboard, as shown on Fig. 1.2D.

Thus, the body of your harp is virtually finished. It only needs varnishing and decorating, and this will be dealt with at a later stage. It remains to drill the string holes right through the soundboard, and this can be done with a hand-drill. If your harp is Paraguayan or Celtic, you can now make the feet and screw them under the base as in Fig. 1.8, but do not use glue as the back feet may need readjusting for balance when the harp is finished. If your choice was a Minstrel harp, a base and a base plate must be made as described in Fig. 1.8, as only then can the feet be screwed.

METHOD OF CONSTRUCTION No. 2

This is the method proposed by W. D. Gollop in a series of articles he wrote for the *Woodworker* magazine in October and November 1968. The cross section of the sound box, or body, is semicircular. It is made in segments, like coopered work and there are eleven segments in all.

The following timber is required.

No. req'd	Description	Long	Wide	Thick	Material
12	Strips for skin	1100	60	6	Parana or agba
1	Base and top	500	500	20	Blockboard
1	Sheet of veneer	1100	300		Mahogany
1	Strip	1100	40		Formica sheet

The above list gives 12 strips for the skin, only 11 are required, but a spare one may be needed in case of mishap.

The author describes the construction as follows:

The work will be facilitated by making a jig or mould (see Fig. 1.9). This may be made from any timber, screwed and glued together firmly enough to hold the segments of the soundbox in place.

Fig. 1.9

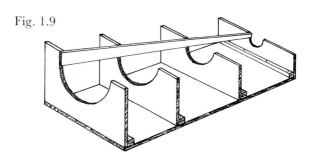

Saw and plane the eleven segments until they fit snugly into the jig. Care must be taken to ensure that the joints are suitable for rubbed jointing. With a light coloured wood, the glue line can best be disguised, and the general appearance of the job enhanced, by the insertion of a contrasting coloured veneer between the box segments as in

Fig. 1.10

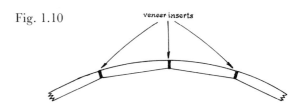

Fig. 1.10. To secure the segments in position, we suggest driving a thin panel pin through the segments and into the frames of the jig. Do not drive them in completely so that when the glue has hardened, the panel pins can be extracted. Now take the soundbox off the jig, handling it with great care. Place it open side down on the bench and set out the oblique base cut, which is 58° in our case. With a coping saw, cut the base along this line, and replace the soundbox into the jig.

Now fit the baseboard against the bottom of the soundbox, and with a pencil scribe carefully around the inside. Draw another pencil line 5mm outside, and cut the base along this second line in order to have enough wood to allow for the bevel. With a jig saw, cut out the round hole in the base. Glue the baseboard into position, and secure it with thin panel pins and proceed in the same manner for the top of the soundbox.

With the jig, baseboard and top combining to take the strain from the joints, a start can be made on cleaning up the inside of the box. You can choose at this stage to leave the interior segmented, which means that only the surplus glue need be cleaned off, but I favour the idea of having the inside of the box rounded to match the exterior, as I gather that the rounded interior is musically more desirable. A curved scraper such as that produced by "Sandvik" is useful for this interior shaping. After scraping the interior, cut strips of glass fibre tape 25mm wide, coat all internal joints with resin, let it gel, and cover all joints with tape. When the first coat of resin is set apply a second coat, but without tape this time. This will reinforce the body considerably.

The sound holes at the back can be marked and cut out at this juncture. After a final clean up, the side rails can be glued, and two coats of white polish can be applied to the interior. The body is now ready to receive the soundboard and to do this, proceed in the same way as described in Method No. 1.

METHOD OF CONSTRUCTION No. 3

The body of your harp can be made of reinforced glass fibre. This most versatile material is quite suitable for the job, but it can only be used for the skin, as the soundboard must be made of wood. A harp maker from the USA, Earl Thompson, of Silver Spring, Maryland, used to make the whole body in glass fibre, soundboard included, but these

harps are at present no longer in production. A
wooden soundboard undoubtedly gives a better
tone.

To make the skin in glass fibre, it is necessary at
first to make two moulds. The first mould is made
all of wood, and is described in Fig. 1.11; this is a
female mould. The second mould (*male*) is made of
reinforced glass fibre.

First make mould No. 1 as described in Fig. 1.11.
Any close grained timber will do, provided it is free
of knots. The mould itself is mounted on a base of
blockboard. The outside of this mould must be
made with great care, scraped, glasspapered,
button polished, glasspapered again, and French

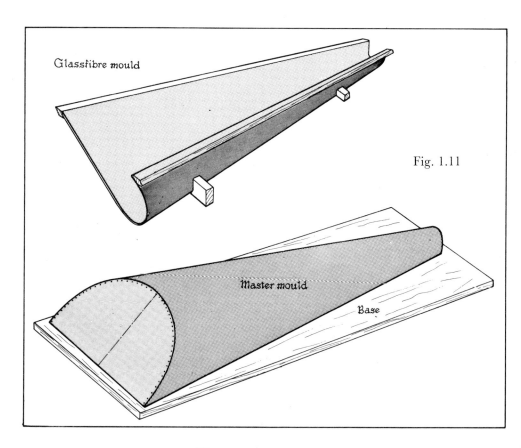

Glassfibre mould

Fig. 1.11

Master mould

Base

polished. Then it is coated with a polish containing a good proportion of carnauba wax, buffed with a soft cloth, and waxed again six times. This wax coating serves as a parting or release agent to which the resin will not adhere.

The amateur harp maker will be well advised to read the book *Glass Fibre for Amateurs* by G. M. Lewis and R. H. Warring, published by Model and Allied Publications Ltd. The reader will appreciate that it is beyond the scope of this book to describe the technique of working with glass fibre and we shall only deal with the parts which are essential to our subject.

Of course, it takes longer to make one harp in glass fibre than it takes to make one all in wood, but once the final mould is made it is quick and easy. Several harp bodies can be made from the same mould and the job looks really professional. The book we recommend is ideal for the amateur, because it eliminates the need for expensive equipment and ensures that the end product will be reliable.

Materials required for Method No. 3 are as follows:

6lb. of clear resin,
1lb. of gel coat resin,
1lb. of release wax (*Slipwax*),
8oz. of colouring pigment (British racing green),
6yd. of open weave glass fibre,
1 eight oz. bottle of catalyst (hardener),
1 pint of acetone for cleaning brushes.

When the female wooden mould is made, you can make the male mould from it as shown in Fig. 1.11. Mould No. 1 may now be discarded. It is advantageous to reinforce the outside of Mould No. 2 with battens and strips of glass fibre and resin; a mould made this way will last a long time. Apply several coats of release wax on the inside as you did for the female mould.

To make the skin, the resin must be pigmented "British racing green" colour, or black. First apply the pigmented gel coat. Let it become tacky and lay on it some open-weave glass cloth, then apply more resin with a stippling action of the brush until the cloth is saturated. Air bubbles trapped under the cloth must be removed by further stippling action of the brush, or by using a special roller. Place another layer of cloth over the first, and soak it again with resin; a third layer of cloth should be applied in the same way. Each coat of resin sets in about 30 minutes. Trim the edges with a sharp knife before the resin is cured, and unmould after about three hours. Put the skin back into the mould in order to prevent any distortion during the curing process.

Now fit the baseboard against the bottom of the soundbox as previously described. With a sharp pencil scribe carefully around the inside; draw another line 5mm outside the first, and cut the base along this second line, so that you have enough wood left to accommodate the bevel. Cut

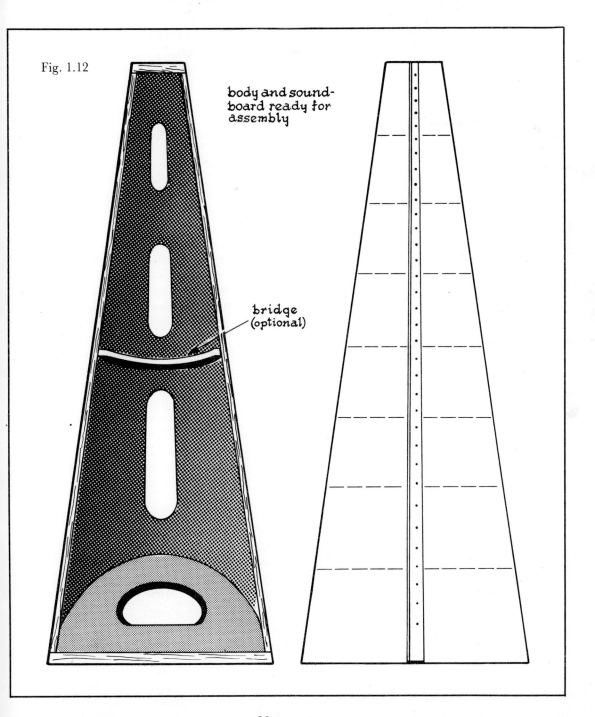

Fig. 1.12

body and sound-
board ready for
assembly

bridge
(optional)

33

the round hole in the base and bevel the edges to fit snugly inside the skin.

When the fitting is good, coat the bevelled edges with plenty of resin. Take the skin out of the mould and secure the base to the skin with panel pins, starting at the middle, one panel pin every 30mm. Prepare the top piece and secure it in position with panel pins and resin. Prepare the side rails and fix them along the sides with more resin and panel pins. When the resin is fully cured, the whole structure will be very strong and there will be no need for frames to strengthen it.

Now, with a sharp awl and a template made of stiff card, scribe the three elongated soundholes at the back and cut them out with an electric jig saw or a new key-hole saw. Glasspaper the edges, and brush a coat of resin over them in order to cover up loose fibres. Apply one more coat of green resin over the inside. Smooth the outside with very fine "wet and dry" abrasive paper, then with a rubbing compound, so that the skin is ready to receive one final coat of cellulose paint from an aerosol can (B.M.C. Dark British racing green). This final touch is done when the harp is finished because there are still a lot of things to do which could spoil the lacquer. The skin is now ready to receive the soundboard, and this may be secured in the same manner as already described for the two previous methods of construction.

CHAPTER 2
THE CELTIC HARP

To make the neck and pillar of the Celtic harp, the following timber is required:

No. req'd	Description	Long	Wide	Thick	Material
1	Plank for neck	700	210	18	Mahogany, oak or sapele.
1	Plank for neck	1400	210	12	,,
1	Plank for pillar	1100	170	18	,,
2	Planks for pillar	1100	170	12	,,

The reader will notice that the neck and pillar are made of laminated timber which prevents them from warping under stress. The part of the neck which is jointed to the top of the body needs building up, and a shoulder is carved as shown in

Fig. 2.1

CELTIC HARP

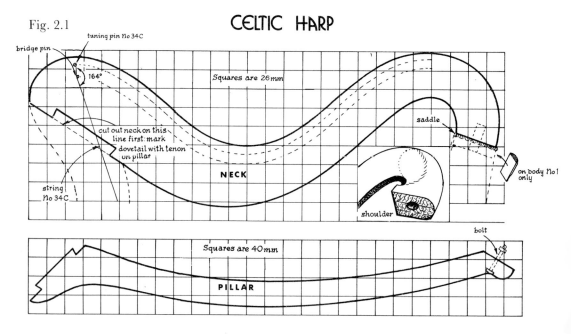

tuning pin No 34C

bridge pin

164°

Squares are 26mm

cut out neck on this line first: mark

dovetail with tenon on pillar

NECK

saddle

on body No 1 only

string No 34C

shoulder

bolt

Squares are 40mm

PILLAR

Fig. 2.1. This is best done with a rasp and gouge. Make a tracing of the neck and pillar on transparent drawing paper, Fig. 2.1. Transfer the tracing to your timber by means of carbon paper, then cut to shape, preferably with a bandsaw. The joint between pillar and neck can either be a dovetail joint, or it can be secured with two 12mm dia dowels. If the dovetail joint has been chosen, it is necessary to account for the length of the tenon before cutting the timber to shape, this tenon being 15mm long. When all the timber is cut out, glue the three pieces together and clamp overnight then remove excess glue and glasspaper.

The base of the pillar is secured to the body by means of a carriage bolt and the hole for this should be drilled as near as possible to the base frame so that the nut can be tightened from inside.

It is an advantage not to join up the pillar and neck permanently at this stage. If the joints were made true, the harp can be assembled and even strung temporarily in order to mark the holes for the tuning blades. In any case, the only joint that needs glueing later is the one between the neck and pillar. The other joints (the neck to the top and the pillar to the base) are better left dry, that is to say without any glue: these two joints are not square. Pillar and neck are slightly out of upright, two degrees to the left (see end of chapter 3). A harp made this way can easily be dismantled for repairs or adjustments, whereas if it were glued it would be impossible.

Do not forget the little saddle between shoulder and body which provides an easy means for registration of the two parts. Next, drill the holes for the tuning pegs. Use a bit of the same size as the small ends of the tuning pegs. By means of a

Templates for neck and pillar of Celtic harp

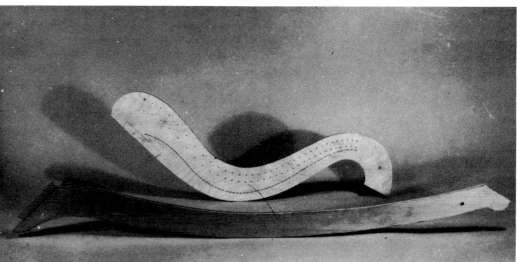

Fig. 2.2

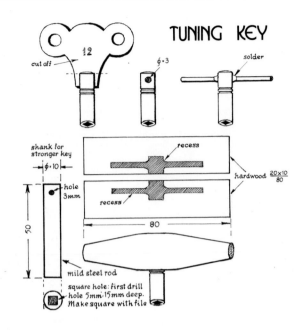

Fig. 2.3

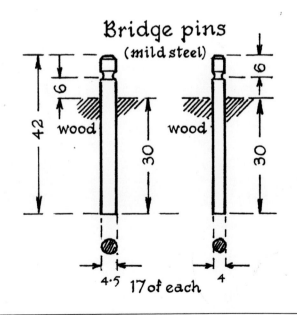

taper pin hand reamer held in a wrench, enlarge the holes from the back of the neck so that each tuning peg fits and protrudes by the same amount. This can be done by wrapping a piece of masking tape over the reamer at the point where it must not go any further in the wood. The reamer is very sharp, and it is very easy to make the hole too big.

In order to obtain a good fit for the tuning pegs the reader will be well advised to make the tuning key and use it to push the tuning pegs in and out of their holes. How to make the tuning key is fully described in Fig. 2.2.

The bridge pins consist of short lengths of steel rod with circular recesses or notches for the strings, which are to ensure that all strings are on the same plane. Two sizes of steel rod are used for making them as illustrated in Fig. 2.3. The holes for the bridge pins are not drilled right through the neck: leave about 5mm before the drill goes through. The notches for the string should protrude 10mm from the neck.

In the past, harps were always decorated, and great importance was attached to their adornment: oral and visual pleasure "greatly delighted the ear and highly relaxed the spirit . . ." During the Rococo period the craze for decoration was such that the soundboard often disappeared under a mass of exuberant strands of vegetation, patches of blossoming flowers and miniature landscape paintings. During the Napoleonic era, the passion for Roman antiquities assumed exaggerated proportions. Classical and Egyptian emblems were copied, modelled in "Compo" and glued on capitals, pillars, necks, and bases; all these ornaments were gilt and burnished. These trends persisted up until the end of the nineteenth century.

Modern concert harps have little or no decorations at all, but the amateur harp maker should not disregard ornamentation, because there is no such thing as a "modern" Folk harp. In our opinion, the Celtic harp and the Minstrel harp should be decorated. Traditionally, Celtic harps were adorned with designs reminiscent of those found in ancient manuscripts such as the Book of Kells, the Book of Durrow or the Book of Lindisfarne. These beautiful books were written by

Fig. 2.4

Design for bottom of soundboard

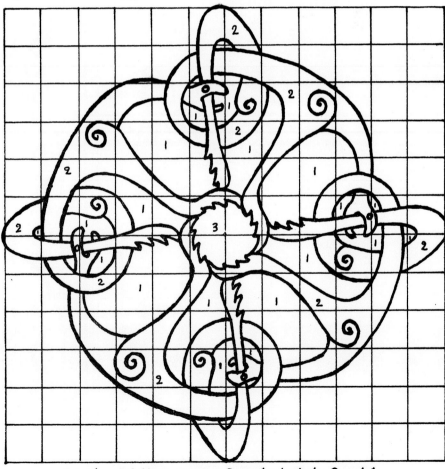

1. pale viridian green 2. pale brick 3. gold

Fig. 2.5

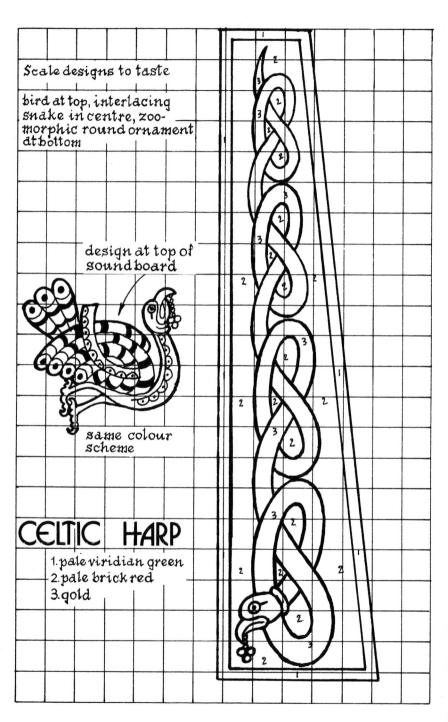

Scale designs to taste

bird at top, interlacing
snake in centre, zoo-
morphic round ornament
at bottom

design at top of
sound board

same colour
scheme

CELTIC HARP

1. pale viridian green
2. pale brick red
3. gold

monastic scholars from the seventh to the tenth centuries, being copies of the gospels which were used in monasteries as reference books. The title pages and the first letter of each chapter were superbly decorated and illuminated with intricate interlacing patterns and strange zoomorphic motifs based on the distorted shapes of animals, birds, and reptiles. This particular style of decoration is now known as Celtic or Pictish Art, and the reader will find an example in Fig. 2.5.

The Minstrel harp lends itself to two types of decoration: the Rococo style and the more popularly developed Folk Art consistent with the taste and traditions of the country where the amateur harp maker lives. Decoration is not essential to the harp's musical function, but because it contributes to the study and enjoyment of decorative crafts, it should be our concern.

When the design has been chosen, it should be drawn full size to fit the soundboard, and should be

Fig. 2.6

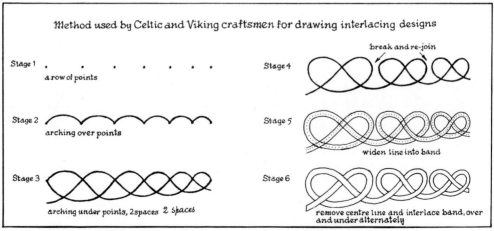

43

Fig. 2.7

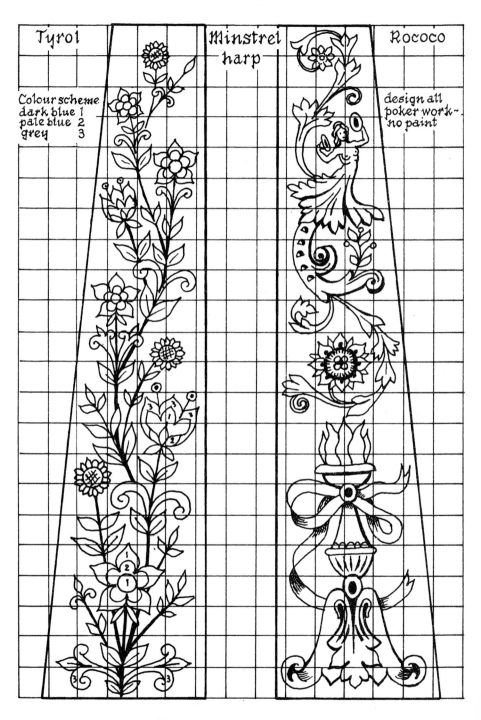

Tyrol

Colour scheme
dark blue 1
pale blue 2
grey 3

Minstrel
harp

Rococo

design all
poker work~
no paint

made on best quality transparent paper, being then transferred to the soundboard with carbon paper. Having traced one side, reverse the drawing and transfer it to the other side of the soundboard. Make corrections with a pencil if necessary.

At this stage you have the choice of using artist's oil colours alone, or better still, to go over your first tracing with a thin red hot poker and score it so that it will appear almost in low relief when it is finished. Electric pokers known as "Pyrographs" are specially made for this work and may be purchased in art shops, the temperature of the stylus being controlled by a thermostat. They are very easy to operate, however. Should the "Pyrograph" be unobtainable, paint the outline of your design in black enamel and let it dry. What has been said only applies to Celtic and Rococo designs, but Folk floral patterns should be painted according to the colour scheme which suits them best.

Whatever the design, it will be enhanced by a certain amount of gilding. Gilding is a delicate business which calls for a great deal of patience, but the results amply repay the pains taken. It is a very ancient craft which originated as far back as 4000 BC and it has remained fundamentally the same ever since. The gold leaves used for gilding are extremely thin (one 250,000ths of an inch) and the final task of beating the gold to this thickness is all the hand work of skilled craftsmen who manage to beat the precious metal free from cracks, small holes and other blemishes or faults. Gold leaf is sold in "books" of 25 leaves, termed *loose leaf*, or *transfer*. The former, as the name indicates, is free between leaves of tissue paper. The transfer is the same gold as the loose (25 sheets) except that each leaf is attached to the tissue paper by a film of wax for easy handling.

Loose leaf is difficult to handle and if your wife opens the door of the workshop to say that you are wanted on the telephone, the draught will make the gold leaf airborne to vanish instantly . . . !

Transfer gold leaf is a bit more expensive but more manageable for amateur gilders, while the tools used in gilding are neither numerous nor expensive.

Two methods are used: water gilding and oil gilding. Water gilding may be burnished with an agate burnisher and made extremely bright, while oil gilding is smoothed down with a pad of silk cloth 24 hours after the application of the gold leaf and then given a coat of colourless lacquer, the final result being quite satisfactory.

Whatever the method, the most important thing is that the wood grain must be made very smooth and coated with "gesso". This is a preparation used for some thousands of years by artists and craftsmen alike all over the world. It is the only suitable ground for tempera painting and it consists of gilder's whiting, rabbit skin glue and a few drops of boiled linseed oil. It can be purchased in good art shops and directions for use are supplied with the whiting and size.

Briefly, the first task is to prepare the rabbit skin size in a glue pot or double walled saucepan, add some cold water, stir and allow to stand overnight. Warm to 65° C (150° F), and stir until dissolved. Do not boil. Add the gilder's whiting and mix well together with a piece of wood to get rid of all lumps, when the gesso should have the consistency of ready-mixed paint. Add two or three drops of linseed oil and stir well. Keep the preparation warm, and it is ready for use.

Apply it to the wood with a hog-hair brush, preferably a flat one. For oil gilding four coats of gesso are required, while for water gilding it is necessary to apply eight coats. Though each coat must be dry before the next is laid, *all coats must be completed in one day*. If they are laid properly, nothing needs to be done to the final coat. Gesso, by its nature, is very smooth, but nothing must be left on the ground that would irritate or tear the gold, which, it will be remembered, is only 1/250,000th part of an inch thick. If the surface is not perfect, gently rub flour glass paper on the rough parts. If too much gesso has come to rest in the hollows and other parts it must be removed with a modelling tool or an old piece of linen dipped in water. This has to be done very carefully, bearing in mind that the gesso surface must be retained.

The next stage is to apply Armenian bole to the surface if a really bright surface is aimed at, but this is not essential. The Armenian bole can be replaced by one coat of Lefranc "Mixtion à dorer" which is an orange coloured oil gold size ready for use and available from gilding supply shops. Stir the size well, and with a flat hogbrush go over the surface thoroughly, making sure all is covered. Ensure, too, that the surface is covered with the minimum amount of gold size. This must be stressed, because any suggestion of a puddle in the hollows or surplus on the higher parts will cause uneven dry-outs. Furthermore, if the gold leaf is put on such surfaces, it would never be permanent.

Cover up the work after sizing to prevent dust sticking, and from time to time test for tackiness by touching the gold size lightly with the finger, until it almost holds the finger in position (12 to 18 hours). The drier the better.

Gold leaves are fairly expensive. Each book of 25 leaves 80mm by 80mm costs between 80p to £1.25 (1972). There is a much cheaper substitute called "Dutch leaf" in the trade and these are sold in larger books 140mm square and cost about 50p each. They are copper leaves which are coated with gold by the action of zinc fumes. The method of application is the same as for gold leaf and it is very difficult to notice the difference. A few months after application, Dutch (or Schlag) leaf tends to darken if it is not protected with a coat of colourless lacquer or polyurethane varnish. In any case, the finished result is vastly superior to what may be achieved with spraying gold paint from an aerosol container.

Real gold or Dutch gold will make a really

professional job, but we do not recommend the use of loose gold leaf or loose Dutch leaf if you have no previous experience of gilding. Transfer gold is very easy to apply, as the leaves can be handled and pressed on with the fingers on the tacky gold size. A good tool for the job is what the gilders call a "bob", which consists of a round pad of chamois leather filled with cotton wool, used to settle the gold leaf in its final position. When the area to be gilded has been covered with gold, any little areas left uncovered can be filled with left over offcuts.

The final smoothing down is best done with a silk cloth, 24 hours after the application of the gold leaf, when the size is in its final stage of hardening. The smoothing down is best described as a half-patting, half-stroking motion, the aim being to create a perfectly even and smooth skin of gold. When you are gilding small areas within a painting, such as may happen on the soundboard, it is not essential to have a gesso foundation under the gold size, but the wood grain must be filled somehow. Therefore, apply a thin coat of shellac to the part to be gilded, and when dry, rub with flour glasspaper, twice. Now you may apply the French gold size to the small areas and proceed as previously described.

CARVINGS

Some carving may be done on the neck, pillar, capital and base. An alternative to real carving is the gilder's "Compo" used in the eighteenth century by the Adams brothers. Concert harp ornaments of the Grecian and Gothic types were made in moulded compo, and it is still used in the manufacture of picture frames. It is sold by the pound and is not expensive.

It can be made easily, and here is the recipe:
1: Dissolve and heat $\frac{1}{4}$lb of Scotch glue in a quart of water.
2: Boil together $\frac{1}{4}$ of a gill of turpentine, $\frac{1}{2}$lb of resin and $\frac{1}{4}$ of a pint of boiled linseed oil. (Not on a

naked flame please, or you will most certainly require the fire brigade to come to your assistance!).
3: Boil together preparation No. 1 and No. 2 and simmer for $\frac{1}{4}$ of an hour.
4: Turn out into a bed of whiting until it has the appearance of dough ready for the oven after kneading it with your hands.

Compo is pressed in plaster moulds made from carved wooden masters, and the ornaments are then glued on the wood with Scotch glue. In other words, compo is very useful when several identical decorations are required, but for the amateur who wants to make only one harp it is not worth the bother, straightforward carving being better and more satisfying.

The carving on the Celtic harp must be related to the painted decoration of the soundboard, and this applies also to the Minstrel harp. A good example of carving suitable for the front pillar of a modern Celtic harp may be seen on the Queen Mary harp now in the National Museum of Antiquities, Edinburgh. According to tradition, the instrument was in the possession of Mary, Queen of Scots, when she was on a hunting trip in the Perthshire highlands in 1563. The queen is said to have taken this occasion to present the harp to a Beatrice Gardyn of Banchory (later Mrs. Farquharson of Invercauld).

At a later date, the marriage of a female descendant of Beatrice brought the harp into the Robertson family, of Lude, Perthshire. The instrument remained in the same family until about 1904 when it was purchased at auction for 850 guineas by the Museum. The soundboard of this precious harp is thought to have been decorated with a portrait of the queen, the arms of Scotland in gold, and a goodly number of valuable jewels . . . these ornaments were, however, stolen or lost during the rebellion of 1745.

The Queen Mary harp has relief carving, incised lines made with the parting tool, and poker work burning. The amateur harp maker would be well

49

advised to take it as a model. One of the interesting features of ancient Celtic harps was the double-headed fish carved on the front pillar and according to legend it represents a mythical salmon, one head listening to the music of this world and the other head looking up, offering it to God.

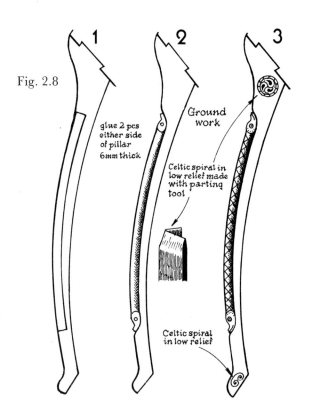

Fig. 2.8

1   2   3

glue 2 pcs
either side
of pillar
6mm thick

Ground
work

Celtic spiral in
low relief made
with parting
tool

Celtic spiral
in low relief

To carve the double-headed salmon on the front pillar, it is necessary to glue some extra wood on both sides of the pillar in order to have a good relief, see Fig. 2.8. Rows of decorative gouge cuts may be done on the inside of the pillar and on the neck and this calls for clean cutting and neatness. The gouge must be extremely sharp and the first incision must be across the grain, while the second

50

runs in to meet the first, so freeing the chip. The row of gouge cuts must be drawn with a pencil first and all cuts must be exactly the same. Celtic spirals in low relief could also be carved at the top of the pillar and at the base. This is best done with a small parting tool.

SCROLLS

As an alternative to a capital on the Minstrel harp, the scroll is very attractive. It also permits a better joint between the neck and the pillar which is an important structural consideration. It is also suitable for the neck of the Paraguayan harp.

The best way to draw a regular scroll or volute, is to apply the method used by the architects of ancient Greece to make the heads of the columns (or capitals) of their Ionic order. It can all be done

Fig. 2.9

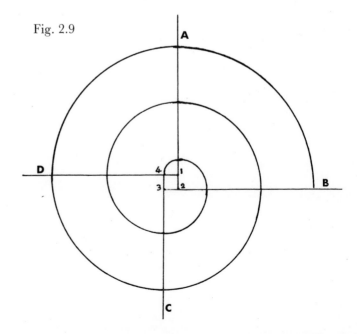

with dividers or compasses, and draw it on transparent paper first and transfer it to the wood by means of carbon paper.

First draw a small square 4mm by 4mm and extend the sides as in Fig. 2.9. Mark the extended

Fig. 2.10

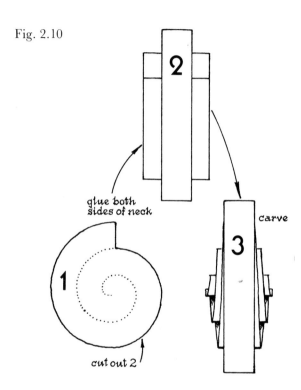

glue both
sides of neck

carve

cut out 2

sides A, B, C, D, and the four corners of the square 1, 2, 3, 4. Put the point of your compasses at corner No. 1 of the small square, open the legs 4mm and draw an arc from corner No. 4 to the extended side A. Open the compasses to 8mm, and place the point at corner No. 2. Draw the arc extended line A to extended line B. Open the compasses to 12mm, place the point at corner No. 3 and draw arc extended side B to extended line C, and so on. The radii are: 4, 8, 12, 16, 20, 24, 28, 32, etc (being an arithmetical progression).

Trace two volutes (one reversed) on two wood blocks, 120mm by 120mm and cut the outline as in Fig. 2.10. Now glue them on the neck so that the end of the spiral may be extended with a pencil line to meet the line of the tuning pegs. When the glue is dry, start work on the dotted line of the spiral with a gouge, taking great care not to touch the line. A fairly flat gouge is used for this grounding and the perpendicular tool cuts must be at least 2mm away from the dotted line. The roughing-in is done with the same flat gouge and the final setting-in with the chisel while the paring along the dotted line is best done at the end.

The important point is that the outside of the spiral should end flush with the wood of the neck in a very gradual curve. It is great fun to make a good scroll, and it does not take very long. On the flat part of the base of the Minstrel harp, two Adam-style acanthus leaves could be glued on after carving. If you do not feel confident enough to tackle two identical acanthus leaves, you may like to know that they can now be purchased in DIY shops ready for application. They are made of plastic, of course, but when they are gilded they are quite effective and should not be frowned on.

CHAPTER 3
THE MINSTREL HARP

Photograph by
Basil Kidd, Deal,
Kent.
Harpist, Rosemarie
Horton

The Minstrel harp differs from the Celtic harp in the shape of its pillar and neck. The pillar is straight and the neck has a more accentuated curve upwards thus making the harp taller. The bass strings are consequently a bit longer, but from the sound point of view there is very little difference between the two.

The straight pillar is made of a piece of well-seasoned timber such as oak, mahogany, or Parana pine, 1070mm long by 40mm wide and 40mm thick. The amateur harp maker can exercise his skill and ingenuity by altering the design of the pillar and capital, as long as the wood is not weakened by excessive carving. The drawing shows a round fluted pillar, but it could be spiralled or carved to personal taste; the same applies to the capital. A volute may be preferred, or the capital may be turned on the lathe and the reader must make his own choice.

It will be noticed, however, that the base of the pillar does not rest on the soundbox, wherein it differs from the Celtic harp. This is a mechanical disadvantage, as the tremendous pull of all the strings under tension tends to lift the soundbox from its base, and in order to prevent this happening, a base plate is essential. The base and base plate must be very strong, glued and screwed together, and to frame E as well. The straight bevelled edge of the base plate carries the load to the base of the soundbox and prevents any likelihood of splitting or rending.

The neck of the Minstrel harp is made of laminated timber in exactly the same way as already described for the Celtic harp, and the amount of timber required is also the same. As the only difference is in the shape of the neck, the reader should follow the description at the beginning of chapter 2 and refer to Fig. 3.1 for differences in measurements. The semitone blades are positioned in the same manner as for the Celtic harp. If a volute is preferred to a capital, the forward part of the neck is slightly extended so that

Fig. 3.1

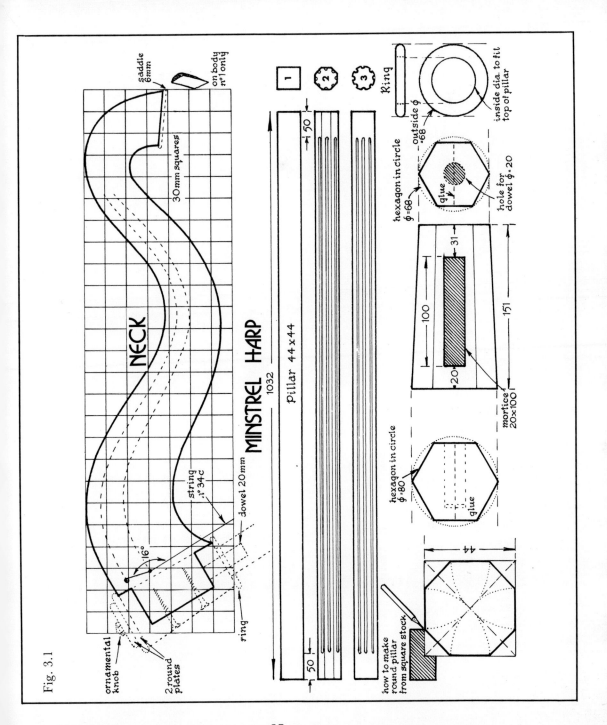

NECK

MINSTREL HARP

30mm squares

saddle 6mm

on body n°1 only

ornamental knob

2 round plates

ring

16°

string n° 34c

dowel 20mm

1032

Pillar 44×44

50

50

Ring

inside dia. to fit top of pillar

outside ⌀ =68

hexagon in circle ⌀=68

glue

hole for dowel ⌀·20

100

31

20

151

mortice 20×100

hexagon in circle ⌀·80

glue

44

how to make round pillar from square stock

The Minstrel Harp
Photograph by Basil Kidd

Minstrel Harp
Neck and Capital

Minstrel harp
Base and base plate

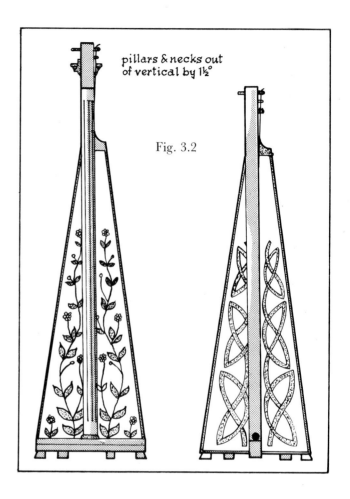

pillars & necks out
of vertical by 1½°

Fig. 3.2

the centre of the volute is perpendicular to the axis of the front pillar. The wood for the volute is glued either side of the neck.

The volute can be carved now, but when it comes to the drilling, a piece of wood must be placed under the neck so that it rests absolutely flat on the plate of the electric drill. Capital, front pillar and base plate are gilded or sprayed with gold paint as a cheaper substitute, while the volute, being the continuation of the neck, is only varnished or waxed.

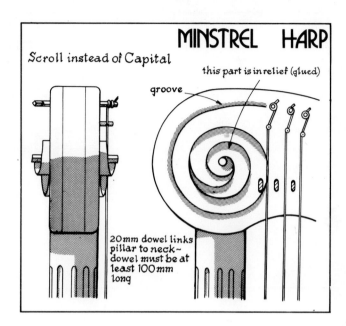

Fig. 3.3

On the Celtic harp and on the Minstrel harp, the pillars are slightly out of upright and this is normal practice for all harps except the types called "perpendicular". The angle out of upright must be such that the strings are perpendicular to the soundboard and it is hardly noticeable: about 2 or 3 degrees to the left. This does not, however, apply to the Paraguayan harp.

CHAPTER 4
THE PARAGUAYAN HARP

"Los Picaflores" (Stars on Sunday, I.T.V.)
Photograph by Harris, Oxford

The Paraguayan harp, as already mentioned, is classified as a "perpendicular" harp, which is structurally stronger than other types. Its only disadvantage is that it cannot produce accidental semitones. Sharps and flats are set before starting to play the tune, and when an accidental occurs, the voice or the guitar does it. As the strings play "open", that is to say, without interference from blades or hooks, the sound is brilliant and clear. The instrument has 36 strings, and on some harps, the lowest string is F, while on others it is C. Some harps are provided with guitar machine heads, others with tapered tuning pegs. We have constructed harps of both types and found that the guitar machine heads present no real advantage, except that it could be argued that they look better. In our opinion they seem to be too sophisticated for a Folk instrument, and Paraguayan harpists appear to be equally divided on the question, some favouring the old tuning peg system, others preferring the guitar machine heads.

For simplicity of construction we have chosen the tuning peg system, and we shall start the work by making a full size drawing of the harp as previously described. Several sheets of drawing paper are fixed to the wall by means of adhesive tape, so that they accommodate the whole profile of the harp. First, draw the line representing the soundboard, at an angle of 57° from the horizontal, as shown in Fig. 1.6. Having done so, draw the neck and front pillar and then make a template of the neck with a piece of plywood or hardboard.

The following timber is required for the neck:

No. req'd	Description	Long	Wide	Thick	Material
1	Sheet of plywood	1000	1000	5	
1	Plank for flanks	1600	250	12	Mahogany, oak.

64

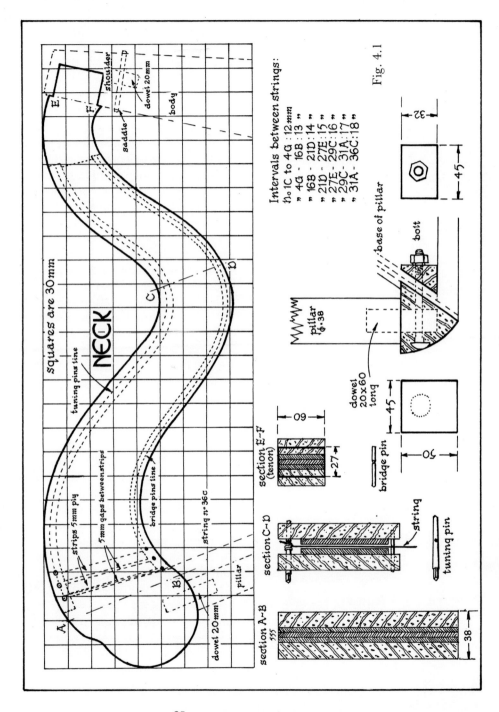

Fig. 4.1

section E-F
(tenor)

section C-D

section A-B
555

Intervals between strings:

h. 1C to 4G : 12mm
" 4G - 16B : 13 "
" 16B - 21D : 14 "
" 21D - 27E : 15 "
" 27E - 29C : 16 "
" 29C - 31A : 17 "
" 31A - 36C : 18 "

squares are 30mm

NECK

tuning pins line

bridge pins line

strips 5mm ply

5mm gaps between strips

dowel 20mm

string n° 36c

dowel 20mm

pillar

shoulder

saddle

body

base of pillar

pillar φ·38

bolt

dowel 20x60 long

bridge pin

string

tuning pin

With your template of the neck, trace the two mahogany flanks and the two plywood plates which are narrower than the flanks in order to make the 20mm groove where the tuning pegs will be secured (see cross section on Fig. 4.1). On the piece of mahogany cut for the back flank (when facing the profile of the harp) mark the positions of all strings, bridge pins and tuning pegs. Drill holes for the tuning pegs and bridge pins.

Now, glue one plywood plate over in position and secure it with a few panel pins. Do not drill the front piece of mahogany at this stage, but simply glue the plywood plate to it as before. On the first plate (the mahogany flank and plywood plate glued together) drill bridge pin holes. Now, on the plywood plate, draw the string lines again, so that each line is adjacent to the front of the bridge pin hole and the back of the tuning peg hole. Cut strips of plywood and glue them either side of the string pencil lines so that they are arranged as in Fig. 18. They make grooves for the harp strings to reach the tuning pegs.

Then, glue the other plywood plate to the front flank of mahogany and secure it in position with a few panel pins. Finally, glue all the parts together, cramp them and leave overnight. Drill the tuning peg holes right through, but for the bridge pin holes do not extend the holes quite right through; leave about 5mm as it looks better.

The next step is to taper the holes for the tuning pegs with a reamer $\frac{9}{32}$in. ($5\frac{5}{8}$in. overall). The tuning pegs should be sawn off at the thin end so that they only protrude about 5mm from the front of the neck. Now, with all tuning pegs in position and looking from above, mark the holes (2mm dia) which are drilled through the pegs in order to anchor the string ends. It is better to drill these holes not quite opposite the channels for the strings. The strings should take about three turns on the pegs before going through the channels, and in order to account for this, drill the 2mm holes near the mahogany front flank.

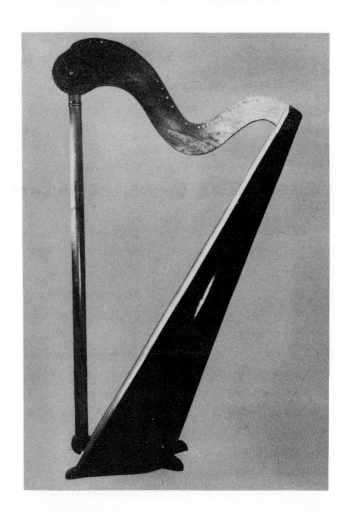

Paraguayan harp
before stringing

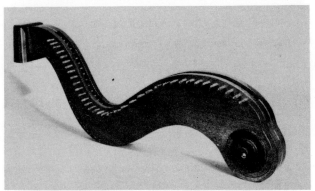

Paraguayan harp
Neck and shoulder

67

Paraguayan harp.
Neck and support
for semitone systems

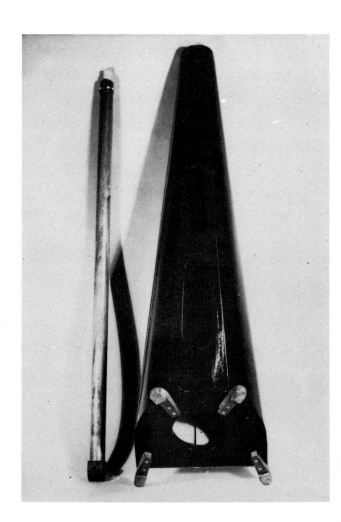

Paraguayan harp.
Pillar and back
view of "body"

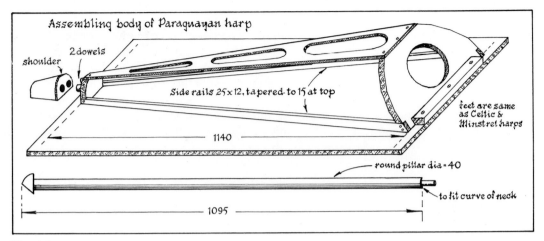

Fig. 4.2

Fig. 4.3

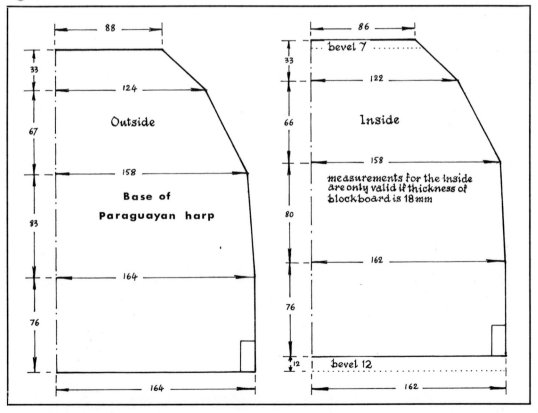

The bridge pins can now be made according to Fig. 4.1 and gently hammered in their respective holes. The circular notches for the strings should all be visible from underneath at the lower ends of the channels. The front part of the neck may be decorated with some marquetry or carving; a circular design would be the most suitable, just above the front pillar. Upholstery brass nails may also be used as ornaments. The reader will have noticed that there is a tenon at the thin end of the neck which secures the neck to the shoulder. This may now be constructed according to Fig. 4.1.

THE BODY

This part of the harp is very simple to make, and the drawing in Fig. 4.2 is self-explanatory. The following timber is required:

No. req'd	Description	Long	Wide	Thick	Material
1	Bottom and top	450	300	20	Blockboard
2	Rails for sides	1200	25	12	Ramin, agba
1	Back	1200	200	12	Plywood, ramin or agba
8	Skin	1200	70	6	Ramin or agba
2	Planks for soundboard	1200	150	10	Spruce
2	String bars	1200	30	10	Spruce

The first thing to do is to draw the outline of the base directly on the piece of hardboard. The first drawing is, of course, the OUTSIDE outline shown in Fig. 4.2. As for the INSIDE, you draw this later, when the base is cut out. The top piece is then prepared in the same way.

The bevels must be cut with great care, so that the skin will fit with the minimum need for correction. Next, prepare the two side rails which are tapered from 25mm at the base to 15mm at the top. Secure the base to the bench between two bevelled rails, at an angle of 57° as shown in Fig. 4.2 and screw and glue the side rails in the notches of the base and top. Prepare the back, fix it in position with screws only, but do not bevel it yet.

The segments for the skin are cut out in pairs, starting with the pair over the side rails. The top edges of this first pair of segments may be left square, but subsequent ones should be bevelled as in coopering work. Make the segments a bit longer than needed, by about 5mm each end, and glue them in position and secure with panel pins. Strips of contrasting veneer between segments enhance the general appearance and hide the glue lines.

Paraguayan harps are often painted black, except for the soundboard, in which case there is no need for strips of veneer between segments. The reader can be assured that the sound of the harp will not be affected by paint or varnish.

When you are ready to place the fourth pair of segments, you may unscrew the back and bevel the edges in order to obtain a perfect fit. When you are satisfied that the fitting is good, glue and screw the back on again and fix the last segment. If the joints between segments are not perfect, the inside may be reinforced with glass fibre. The whole structure should now be quite strong and ready to receive the soundboard which is made in the same way as previously described. However, the reader will appreciate that the soundboard of the Paraguayan harp, being longer than those of the Celtic and Minstrel harps, means that a longer jig should be made, and the jig should be 200mm longer at the broad end. For the construction of the soundboard, follow the same method as previously described, but take the measurements from Fig. 4.2.

For the top end of the soundboard a "saddle" should be made. Drill the hole for the dowel in the centre of the saddle, and use it to locate the holes in the shoulder and top piece, but do not glue the saddle because if you have made a mistake, it will show when the strings are under tension. If a little gap can be seen between shoulder and body, the harp should be dismantled and the saddle should be bevelled, or a new one should be made, thinner or thicker as necessary.

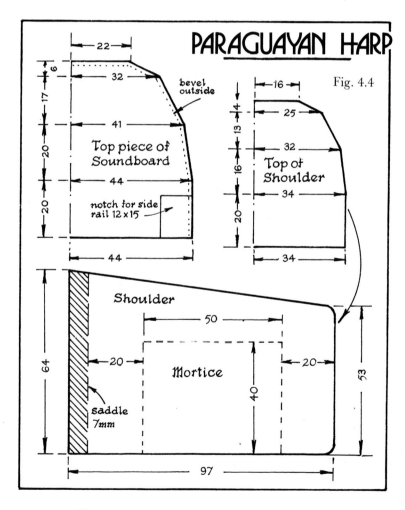

PARAGUAYAN HARP

Fig. 4.4

Top piece of Soundboard

bevel outside

notch for side rail 12 x 15

Top of Shoulder

Shoulder

Mortice

saddle 7mm

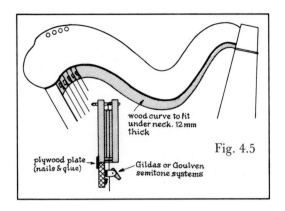

wood curve to fit
under neck. 12 mm
thick

Fig. 4.5

plywood plate
(nails & glue)

Gildas or Goulven
semitone systems

The front pillar: Paraguayan harps have straight, rounded pillars with a ring or two made on a pole lathe, but more often they are left quite plain. The pillar is too long to be turned on an ordinary lathe, so it has to be made by hand. This is much easier than it seems, as the square piece of timber is made octagonal, then gradually planed to the round, using a cardboard template to check for even roundness. The best wood for the front pillar is oak or mahogany, but Parana pine may be used if hardwood is difficult to obtain.

When inserting the top of the pillar in the neck, make it slightly tapered in order to get a good fit. Secure the base of the pillar to the soundbox as shown in Fig. 4.1. Screw the feet under the base plate, and most of the work is done. Give your harp a good finish, and do all the varnishing and painting before stringing. The soundboard should be left plain and be French polished with a transparent shellac.

CHAPTER 5

SEMITONE SYSTEMS

Up to the sixteenth century, all harps were diatonic and could not produce sharps and flats. They were excellent musical instruments as long as the music kept to one key, as was the case for most folk and popular music. As the harp became required for more sophisticated kinds of music in which semitones were necessary, the harp makers of the sixteenth century made harps with a second row of strings alongside the original row; this second row of strings provided the sharps and flats. A better solution was found in Wales, which consisted of sandwiching a row of semitone strings between two outer rows with the normal scale in duplicate. But the Welsh "triple harp" was too difficult to play and it was replaced by the double-action pedal harp invented by a Frenchman, Sebastian Erard, driven from France to Great Britain by the French Revolution. His invention was patented in London in 1792, but the complicated mechanism of the Erard harp is beyond the scope of the amateur harp maker.

The simpler system of hooks invented in the Austrian Tyrol towards the end of the seventeenth century is still used on Folk harps today. At first, not every string was given the advantage of a hook, but now the Minstrel and Celtic harps have hooks on all strings. The Paraguayan harp, however, had remained diatonic, but there is no reason why it should not be modernised. The trouble is that it is a perpendicular harp, and thus cannot receive hooks in the normal way.

We propose one solution to the problem which consists of widening the neck as shown in Fig. 4.5, so that semitone blades, hooks, or levers can be fixed.

Paraguayan harpists will perhaps object to this modification on the grounds that their harps are traditional and should therefore remain as they are.

Basically, there are four types of semitone systems: the hooks, the blades, and the levers. All have their merits and drawbacks. The reader will

75

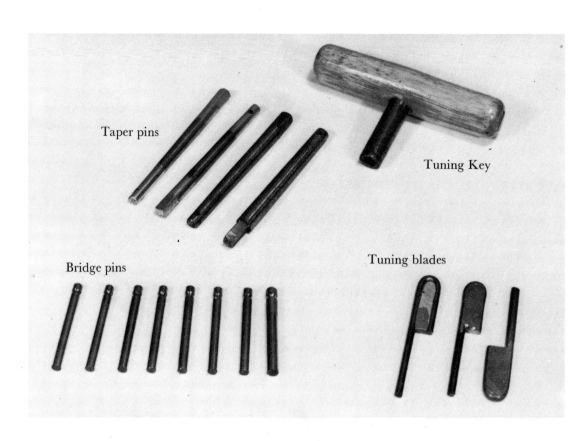

Taper pins

Tuning Key

Bridge pins

Tuning blades

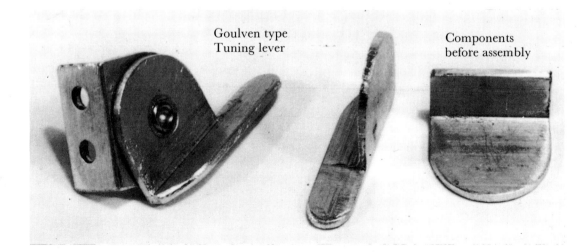

Goulven type
Tuning lever

Components
before assembly

decide which type to select according to available materials, tools and skill, from the simple hook of old to the elaborate Japanese lever system.

A tuning blade, hook or lever shortens the length of the vibrating part of the string and raises its pitch by one semitone. The amount by which the string is shortened is determined by means of a simple calculation based upon the well-tempered scale invented by J. S. Bach, which is now universally recognised. Folk music of eastern countries does not follow this chromatic scale, and bagpipe music does not follow it either . . . that is why there are people who find it difficult to appreciate bagpipe music. They consider that it is completely out of tune, but they are wrong.

The amount by which a string is shortened in

Lever and blade arrangement on Celtic Harp

order to produce a sharp is equal to its vibrating length divided by 17.8, but in practice this factor is regarded as 18. Banjo, guitar and mandoline frets are spaced in this way.

So now, I am afraid, you have to do some arithmetic. If you find mathematical division a bit tedious, you can multiply the vibrating lengths by 0.0555 which gives the same result and is a great deal faster. The results of your calculations will give you the distances beneath the bridge pins where tuning blades should press on the strings in order to make them sound one semitone higher. Mark this position carefully on the wood of the neck, just behind each string. If you provide your

Fig. 5.1

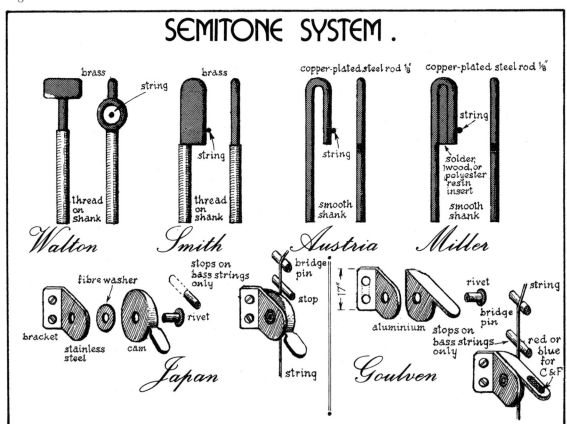

78

harp with semitone hooks for all strings, you will be able to tune it in the key of E flat, and play in eight major and five minor scales when you are used to the instrument. The real beginner should tune his harp in the key of C natural at first, then proceed to the key of F natural. After a few weeks, tune the harp in E flat.

If you have decided to adopt the hook or blade systems, a gauge must be made and it will greatly assist in finding the position of each hole for the axle of the blade or hook. No slackness should be tolerated, but the blade should nevertheless rotate easily. Put some candle wax on the shanks before inserting them in the holes. For the lever system this is not necessary because there are no holes to be drilled, as the lever brackets are simply screwed between the strings. The brackets could be made in stainless steel or aluminium; refer to Fig. 5.2 for measurements. One of the readers of *Woodworker*, Mr. Dennis Miller, has devised a jig for making hooks and we are pleased to illustrate it in Fig. 5.2.

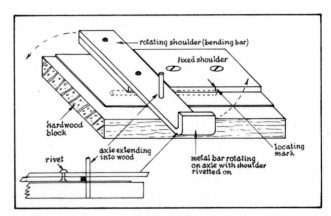

Fig. 5.2

CHAPTER 6
THE BARDIC HARP

The Bardic Harp is derived from the medieval harp of Brian Boru, and it is now at Trinity College, Dublin. This harp is thought to have been made for an Irish king called Brian Boru who was defeated by the Danes near Dublin in 1014, and died of grief soon afterwards. A harp of the same type is housed at the Edinburgh National Museum of Antiquities and according to tradition it belonged to Mary, Queen of Scots.

The bodies of these very old harps were made by hollowing out a solid piece of willow and the cavity at the back was covered by a board. The strings were made of brass or silver, which gave a bell-like tone to the instrument.

In 1933, Arnold Dolmetsch from Haslemere, constructed several little harps of this type and used one of them to decipher the manuscript of Robert ap Huw, thought to contain the earliest examples of Welsh harp music. Robert ap Huw is said to have been a harper at the court of James I, King of Scotland from 1406 to 1437. On the manuscript there is a note in Welsh stating that one particular tune was played at a dinner attended by King Arthur's knights when the salt was ceremoniously placed on the table! The music as deciphered by Arnold Dolmetsch is certainly very fascinating. A young harper from Brittany, Alan Stivel, is successfully reviving the ancient tunes in concert halls, and on the radio and television, playing the tunes of Robert ap Huw even at "pop" festivals . . .!

Like the Paraguayan harp, the Bardic harp is played with the fingernails and not with the fleshy tips of the fingers. The harp is held between the knees, resting on the calves, and with the right foot crossed over the left foot. The technique of playing the wire-strung harp is quite different from that usually advocated for other harps as the fingers are "hooked", and the fingernail is used as a "plectrum". This renders possible various ornaments such as trills, sustained tremolos, and repeated notes which would be impossible on a

81

normal harp. As the left hand is mostly used for chords, the finger tips are used instead of fingernails, and this makes a pleasing contrast in timbre. The fingernails should be cut almost square with the corners slightly rounded off; the correct length is about 3mm beyond the finger tip. If the nail is too long, it will produce a harsh tone. The strings should be pulled gently like those of the classical guitar.

The construction of the Bardic harp does not present any particular problem for the woodworker. The body has a rectangular section somewhat like a box; it is very rigid, and it is not

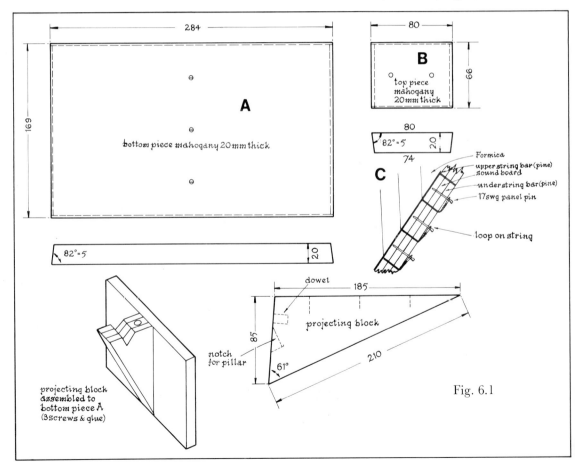

Fig. 6.1

essential to make the front pillar slightly out of upright. In appearance, the Bardic harp is thick-set and stout so no wonder it was chosen for the trade mark of a famous brewer . . .! More than any other harp, the Bardic "clarsach" lends itself to carving and decoration. Before starting the woodwork, first make a full size drawing of the instrument in profile as previously described.

Cut out base of soundbox A and top part B, and cut out and assemble the sides to A and B (resin glue and screws). When the glue is dry, remove the screws and replace them by short pieces of

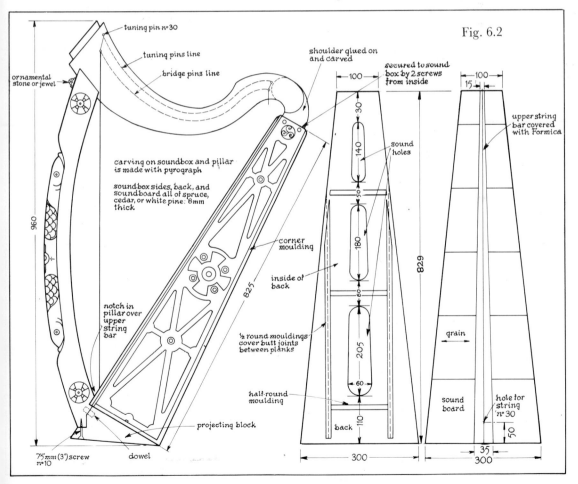

Fig. 6.2

tuning pin nº 30

tuning pins line

bridge pins line

shoulder glued on and carved

secured to sound box by 2 screws from inside

ornamental stone or jewel

upper string bar covered with Formica

carving on soundbox and pillar is made with pyrograph

soundbox sides, back, and soundboard all of spruce, cedar, or white pine: 8mm thick

sound holes

corner moulding

inside of back

notch in pillar over upper string bar

½ round mouldings cover butt joints between planks

grain

half-round moulding

sound board

hole for string nº 30

back

projecting block

75mm (3") screw nº 10

dowel

825

30
140
50
180
60
205
60
110

100
100
15

829

35
300
300

300

50

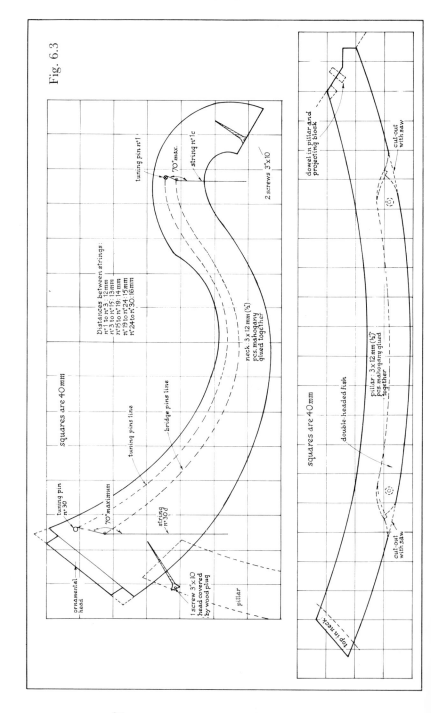

Fig. 6.3

squares are 40mm

tuning pin nº1

tuning pin nº30

70° maximum

70° max.

string nº1c

string nº30

tuning pins line

bridge pins line

Distances between strings:
nº1 to nº3 : 12mm
nº3 to nº15 : 13mm
nº15 to nº19 : 14mm
nº19 to nº24 : 15mm
nº24 to nº30 : 16mm

neck. 3x12mm (½)
pcs. mahogany
glued together

ornamental
head

1 screw 3x10
head covered
by wood plug

pillar

2 screws 3"x10

squares are 40mm

dowel in pillar and
projecting block

cut-out
with saw

pillar : 3x12mm (½)
pcs. mahogany glued
together

double-headed fish

cut-out
with saw

top in neck

dowelling. Prepare the back, and cut out the three slots as on Fig. 6.2. A quarter inch round moulding is glued and pinned to the edges of the sides inside the soundbox. Now glue the back in position with small panel pins. Be careful to drive the panel pins into the edge of the sides and not into the moulding. According to legend, the travelling minstrels of old used the soundbox of their harps as a kind of suitcase! This would suggest that the cavity at the back was covered by a board which could be easily removed.

The next step is to make the neck, the front pillar, and the projecting block. For these, the best plan is to make templates in plywood taken from your full size drawing. On the template for the neck mark the position of the tuning pins and bridge pins. With a 2mm bit, drill through all marks in the template; this will be very useful later as a jig for making the drilling positions on the neck. Note that all drilling should be done before attempting any carving.

The soundboard is made of spruce, Oregon pine, or cedar, in 150mm to 180mm wide strips, with the grain across the table. Apply the same technique as previously described for other harps but do not fix the soundboard yet. This should only be done when neck and pillar are finally screwed and glued. The reason is that the neck is screwed to the top of the sound box from inside. It would be impossible to do so if the soundboard were already fixed. The metal strings are secured to the under string bar in the same way as they are secured on a spinet (see Fig. 6.1C). Each string has a loop at one end, and this loop is hooked to a pin protruding from the under string bar. 17 swg gauge panel pins are used for this, and 5mm of the panel pin should protrude from the wood. The hitching pins are placed halfway between the string holes.

The six bass strings of the Bardic harp are made of acoustic guitar strings, metal wound, 6th, 5th, and 4th. The brass rings which are normally fitted to these strings should be slightly enlarged so that they fit over the heads of the hitching pins. Strings No. 1 to No. 24 are made of phosphor bronze wire, gauged as follows:

No. 1 to No. 4: Gauge 30 (0.315mm)
No. 5 to No. 8: Gauge 28 (0.376mm)
No. 9 to No. 12: Gauge 25 (0.508mm)
No. 13 to No. 16: Gauge 24 (0.559mm)
No. 17 to No. 20: Gauge 23 (0.610mm)
No. 21 to No. 24: Gauge 22 (0.711mm)

String No. 1 should sound D, and the lowest string No. 30 should sound C. Middle C is string No. 16, and it is about 315mm long.

In order that the strings may be recognised, it is essential to paint the heads of the bridge pins and tuning pegs in red or blue (C and F strings). Where the C and F strings enter the upper string bar, it is also a good idea to paint a coloured ring around the holes as it will greatly assist the fingering.

We have designed the Bardic harp so that it may be fitted with gut or nylon strings if so desired. In this case, the upper string (No. 1) will be an F, and the lowest string (No. 30) will be E. The bell-like quality of bronze strings is fascinating at first, but in the long run it tends to become tedious to modern ears. Bronze strings, in our opinion, keep sounding for too long, causing chords to interfere with one another. This undesirable effect would explain why bronze strings were discarded in the past and replaced by gut strings. Another point is that phosphor bronze strings are extremely sensitive to tuning: you turn that tuning key only a quarter turn more than you should, and snap goes the string! A very shattering experience when you are engrossed in the enjoyment of beautiful harmonics: gives you quite a turn!

When gut or nylon strings are used, middle C is string No. 18, and is about 360mm long (string bar to bridge pin). Guitar strings used on the metal strung harp are no longer suitable, as these guitar strings have a steel core and the timbre will not suit the mellow tone of gut strings. Bass strings should be the same as those recommended for the other harps described in this book.

Assuming that you have decided to use phosphor bronze strings, these may be bought ready cut to the right length with the loops ready made, but the amateur harp maker should be able to make the loops himself. However, on no account should the wire be twisted when the loops are being made or your strings will soon snap. Make a winding device as used by spinet makers and described by Geoffrey Gilbert in the magazine *"Woodworker"*, see Fig. 6.4.

The device is cramped to the bench. First, enlist a helper and ask him or her to hold one end of the wire firmly while the other end is passed over the loop of the winding device and gripped in a pair of pliers. Pull both ends of the wire fairly tight and turn the handle 6 to 8 times (maximum), keeping the pair of pliers at a right angle to the length of wire, and allow the end piece to wind itself neatly round the string. Clip off the surplus.

Make sure the soundboard fits nicely over the soundbox, then glue and pin it in position. When you are ready to assemble the neck and pillar to the body, check that the fitting is good everywhere before commencing decoration and carving. It is a good idea to assemble the three main parts of the harp dry, i.e. using screws only, no glue.

Fig. 6.4

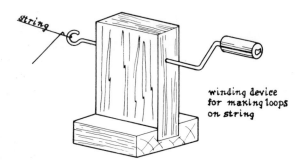

winding device for making loops on string

Fig. 6.5

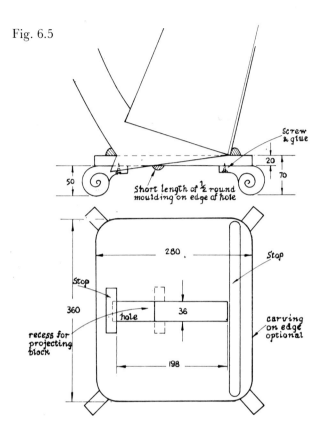

Having made sure that there are no appreciable gaps anywhere, dismantle the harp and start working on the decoration; for guidance, the reader should refer to the chapter on carving and gilding.

Stringing the Bardic harp is quite simple, but it must be done gently, because metal strings are very responsive to changes of tension. Take string No. 1 and pass the loose end of the string through the elongated hole at the back and through the string hole in the soundboard. Pull the string out and secure the loop over the hitching pin; pull tight. Thread the loose end through hole in tuning pin and over bridge pin. Pull tight and cut the string about 35mm above the tuning pin. Loosen the string and bend the end part (about 10mm) away from you at right angles to the hole in tuning pin. Holding the tuning key in your right hand, place it over the square end of the tuning pin and turn it away from you and at the same time hold the string with your left hand in order to prevent it from escaping from the hole in the tuning pin. Test the sound of your string from time to time until it is up to pitch. Proceed in the same way with all strings. The writer is in favour of leaving the strings under tension for two or three days before attempting the final tuning.

SEMITONE SYSTEMS

It is not essential to provide the Bardic harp with semitone blades or cams, and some players prefer to play with "open" strings as did the troubadours in days of yore, but there is no doubt that semitones systems make the Bardic harp a much better musical instrument and the reader should refer to the chapter dealing with the matter.

STAND

The Bardic harp is not provided with feet, but we have placed the centre of gravity so that the harp can stand on the projecting block and the back end of the soundbox. If a more secure stand is required, it is better to make the little stool described in Fig. 6.5.

AMPLIFIER

Though it may appear heretical to provide a medieval musical instrument with an amplifier, there is no reason why the music lover in search of new sounds should not do so. The Bardic harp lends itself very well to this modern treatment. If the harp is to be played in a group it would hardly be heard without an amplifier, but by attaching a guitar microphone to the soundboard, the little harp of Robert ap huw may become the leading instrument of the group! The sound effects possible are really astounding.

CHAPTER 7
STRINGING AND TUNING

Harp strings are made of sheep's gut or nylon monofilament. There are differences of opinion among harpists as to the merits of gut strings over those made of nylon. Nylon strings produce a somewhat metallic sound, while gut strings give a more mellow subdued sound. Nylon strings were much cheaper when they were first introduced, but the price has increased and there is now little difference between the two. Nylon strings have a high tensile strength and good resistance to abrasion, but a new nylon string does not stay in tune for very long. When it has settled it stays in tune more consistently. Gut strings tend to fray before they break and so the harpist is given a warning, but nylon strings snap unexpectedly. Everything considered, gut strings are still preferable.

The Greek philosopher Pythagoras, in about 500 BC, discovered that the musical scale was closely related to mathematics. Plucking a taut string sounding C for instance, he noticed that another string twice as long and equally taut, sounded a note just one harmonic octave below the first. Starting with any string, you could go down the scale by increasing its length according to simple fractions. So, 16/15 of a C string would give the next lower note B, 6/5 of that B note would give A, 4/3 of it would sound a G, 3/2 of that G would give F, 8/5 of F gives E, 16/9 of E gives D, and exactly twice the first C gives C again, one octave lower. Pythagoras' experiment is only valid with strings of the same gauge and equally taut. If a harp were made that way, it would be too tall, and almost impossible to play. By having strings of different gauges musical instruments are easier to handle. The correct gauging of strings is very important, and is determined by complicated calculations beyond the scope of this book.

The gauge of the strings is very important, as each string has a different gauge, and it must be of even thickness throughout its entire length. They are graded with great precision and cannot be mass-produced like fishing lines! The correct grading is as follows:

String number	String notation	Diameter millimetres
1	A	0.60
2	G	0.64
3	F	0.66
4	E	0.68
5	D	0.70
6	C	0.76
7	B	0.80
8	A	0.82
9	G	0.85
10	F	0.92
11	E	0.95
12	D	1.00
13	C	1.05
14	B	1.08
15	A	1.15
16	G	1.20
17	F	1.25
18	E	1.30
19	D	1.35
20	C	1.45
21	B	1.55
22	A	1.65
23	G	1.75
24	F	1.80
25	E	1.85
26	D	1.90
27	C	2.00

Above the gauge of 2mm gut and nylon strings do not produce a clear sound on folk harps, because they are too short, so it is advantageous to have strings metal wound on silk. These strings should be gauged as follows:

String number	String notation	Diameter millimetres
28	B	1.30
29	A	1.40
30	G	1.50
31	F	1.60
32	E	1.70
33	D	1.80
34	C	2.00

The Paraguayan harp has 36 strings, and the two additional strings are at the top, so they are B and C. The gauge of these strings is 0.55 for the B and 0.50 for the top C.

All C strings (Doh) are coloured red; all F strings (Fah) are coloured blue or black; other strings are colourless. Metal strings are silver, except for C and F which are bronze. Octaves are counted from F strings, so that on the Celtic harp, for instance, the first octave will be No. 1-A, No. 2-G and No. 3-F. The second octave will start at No. 4-E down to No. 10-F.

When stringing your harp, you should start with string No. 1 at the top and proceed downwards. If you start with the bass strings you will find that the strings are constantly getting in the way of your fingers. First insert string No. 1 through the top of the soundboard, and pull the string right out of the soundbox through the elongated hole at the back. Make a knot as shown in Fig. 1.2 C. In the knot, insert a short piece of 3rd or 4th octave string. Pull the string back and cut it 50 or 60mm above the top part of the neck. Now thread the loose end through the hole in the tuning pin, and take your tuning key and wind the tuning peg forward. The string should make at least three turns around the pin, and the loose end of the string should be caught under the turns. Don't forget to place the string in the notch of the appropriate bridge pin. Tighten the string and proceed downwards, without attempting to tune the harp at this stage. The thick strings and metal covered strings of the fourth octave downwards do not need to be locked. Leave the strings under tension for an hour or so, then start tuning. Wire bass strings have a loop of silk at one end through which a short wooden peg may be inserted instead of making the normal knot.

The beginner should tune every string to the corresponding note on the piano or pitch pipe, but when the harp is tuned for the first time it is advisable to tune it one complete tone under the normal pitch of the piano. In other words, the C (doh) string of the Folk harp should sound like a B flat on the piano. After a few days, the soundboard will acquire a certain curvature due to the tremendous force exerted by all the strings under tension, and it is then only that the sound of the harp is at its best, and true tuning is easier.

Harps must be tuned frequently because atmospheric conditions constantly affect the tuning and close attention must be paid to this before starting to play, for however excellent the skill of the performer may be, if the tuning is bad, all practice to attain perfection will be of little use.

Beginners should tune their harps with the B tuning blade or lever in the **ON** position and make all strings sound by their normal names in the key of C. When the B tuning blades are turned in the **OFF** position, the vibrating part of the strings are made longer and so the B strings will sound B flat and the harp is in the key of F major. When the instrument is tuned thus it is possible to play in the following key signatures:

F major and D minor: all B tuning blades **OFF**.
C major and A minor: all B tuning blades **ON**.
G major and E minor: all F and B tuning blades **ON** (one sharp).
D major: all B, F, C tuning blades **ON** (two sharps).
A major: all B, F, C, G tuning blades **ON** (three sharps).

E major: all B, F, C, G, D tuning blades **ON** (four sharps).

B major: all B, F, C, G, D, A, tuning blades **ON** (five sharps).

This arrangement gives ten key signatures, which is quite enough for a start. Later on, the new harpist will learn to tune his harp in the key of E^b, which will add B^b, and E^b to the list.

If your new harp is of the Paraguayan type, it should be tuned in the key of C with the help of a piano or a pitch pipe. Now suppose you want to tune your "*Arpa India*" in the key of G, all you have to do is to use your tuning key and wind all F strings a little bit until they sound $F^\#$. If you want to play in the key of F, unwind all B strings and make them sound B^b and so on.

When you are in the process of tuning your harp, never leave the tuning key on the tuning pin, because if it were to fall off from this height it would make an unsightly dent in the soundboard.

CHAPTER 8
ELEMENTARY
HARP PLAYING

Four fingers only are used in playing the harp:
The thumb, called 1,
Index finger, called 2,
Middle finger, called 3, and
Ring finger, called 4.

Irish music publishers still keep numbering the fingers as N. B. Challoner and Boschsa did in the last century, which is as follows:
Thumb: +,
Index: 1,
Middle finger: 2, and
Ring finger: 3.

The little finger is never used, but it must not stick out or curl up, and it moves in sympathy with finger No. 4. Whenever possible, the fingers should be placed on the strings in advance, and this is called: *prepare*. Sit comfortably on a fairly low chair or stool, and place the harp between your legs with the top of the body resting on your right shoulder. Rest your right wrist on the edge of the table, keeping your elbow almost level with it and strike the first chord. To do this, place the fingers of your right hand on strings C, E, G, C (4, 3, 2, 1) as in Fig. 8.1, with the thumb in an upright position. Avoid touching the strings with your nails (these must be cut very short).

Pull the strings gently, one at a time, 4, 3, 2, 1 (see Fig. 8.1) and produce a distinct and equal tone for each. Do not pull the strings all at once or the effect will be spoiled, but play the note in rapid succession and you will produce a typical harp effect. Full chords are always expressed in this manner. When you are able to play the C chord correctly, play the chord of F and then proceed to the chord of G7 (see Fig. 8.3).

The fingers of your left hand (Fig. 8.2), must be placed like those of your right hand, but your wrist must not rest on the edge of the soundboard.. Place finger No. 4 of your left hand on the lowest string C34, and prepare the chord of C with your right hand as before. Strike the chord of C in arpeggio form with your right hand, and at the

Fig. 8.1

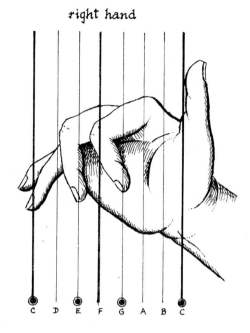

C D E F G A B C

Fig. 8.2

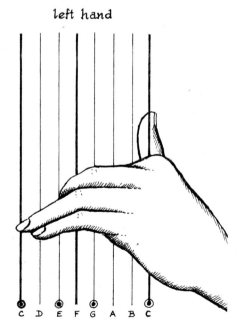

C D E F G A B C

same time strike string 34 with your left hand. Practise this several times; when you can do it easily, proceed with chords of F and G7 as described in Fig. 8.3.

When you begin to play simple tunes, observe the following basic rules:

1: The best fingering for any passage is that which requires the least motion of the hand.
2: Always use the same fingering.
3: When two, three, or four notes of a passage ascend or descend in the same way, the notes must be played with consecutive fingers without leaving one finger between any two others.

Fig. 8.3

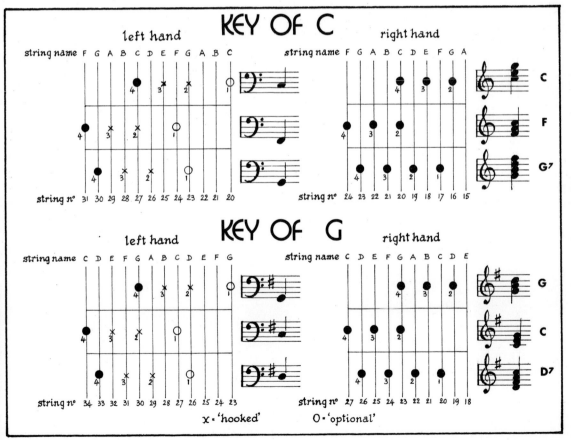

4: When the hand position must be changed, the highest finger when descending (or the lowest when ascending) must be brought on the next string to be struck by passing over the other fingers if the hand descends, or under if the hand ascends.

These rules are fully explained in methods for the harp.

Now, by using the chords in Fig. 8·3, you could already accompany a folk song which uses only two or three chords. Harmonising, as described in text books, sounds alarmingly difficult, but a good simple accompaniment can be adapted to almost any song. A good deal of the music played on the guitar can be played just as well on the Folk harp.

For example, let us sing the song *"Clementine"* with a simple accompaniment on the harp, using only the chords that we know so far. Just play the appropriate chords when you sing the words underlined:

$$\text{Oh my } \frac{\text{darling}}{\text{G}}, \text{ Oh my } \frac{\text{darling}}{\text{G}},$$

$$\text{Oh my } \frac{\text{darling}}{\text{G}} \quad \frac{\text{Clementine}}{\text{D7}}$$

$$\text{Thou art } \frac{\text{lost}}{\text{D7}} \text{ and gone for } \frac{\text{ever}}{\text{G}},$$

$$\text{oh my } \frac{\text{darling}}{\text{D7}} \quad \frac{\text{Clementine}}{\text{G}}.$$

Only two chords of the key of G were used in the song. But now let us try a song in the key of C, which requires more chords, "*There is a tavern in the town*".

There $\frac{is}{C}$ a $\frac{tavern}{C}$ in the $\frac{town}{C}$, $\frac{in\ the\ town}{C}$,

And $\frac{there}{C}$ my $\frac{dear\ love}{C}$ sits him $\frac{down}{G}$, $\frac{sits\ him\ down,}{G}$

And $\frac{drinks}{C}$ his $\frac{wine}{C}$, mid $\frac{laughter}{F}$ $\frac{free}{F}$

And $\frac{never}{G7}$, $\frac{never\ thinks}{G7}$ $\frac{}{C}$ of $\frac{me}{C}$ . . .

Folk harps are easy to play by ear, and now that you have made a start, you will be eager to learn more. Find a harp teacher and take a few lessons: if you fail to find one in your neighbourhood, buy a good method, of which there are many on the market. By the time you are able to play a few tunes, you will already cherish your harp as something precious and very personal.

Recommended methods for the harp:

"*Old tunes for new harpists*" (published by O. Ditson, USA) and available from A. Kalmus Ltd, 38 Eldon Way, Paddock Wood, Tonbridge, Kent.
"*First Tutor for Concert Harp and Clarsach*" by Wilfred Smith. W. Smith, Harp Maker, 15 Castelnau, Barnes, London, SW13 9RP.
"*The New Harp Tutor*" (for Celtic Harp) by S. Larchet and M. Bolger. The Mercier Press, Cork, Ireland.

SEMITONE TABLE
FOR FOLK HARPS

A = Length of string in mm.
B = Distance between bridge-pin and semitone blade or lever

A	B	A	B	A	B	A	B
108	6	333	18·5	558	31	783	43·5
117	6·5	342	19	567	31·5	792	44
126	7	351	19·5	576	32	801	44·5
135	7·5	360	20	585	32·5	810	45
144	8	369	20·5	594	33	820	45·5
153	8·5	378	21	603	33·5	828	46
162	9	387	21·5	612	34	840	46·5
171	9·5	396	22	621	34·5	850	47
180	10	405	22·5	630	35	860	47·5
189	10·5	414	23	639	35·5	870	48
198	11	423	23·5	648	36	876	48·5
207	11·5	432	24	657	36·5	885	49
216	12	441	24·5	666	37	890	49·5
225	12·5	450	25	675	37·5	900	50
234	13	459	25·5	684	38	910	50·5
243	13·5	468	26	693	38·5	920	51
252	14	477	26·5	702	39	930	51·5
261	14·5	486	27	711	39·5	940	52
270	15	495	27·5	720	40	950	52·5
279	15·5	504	28	729	40·5	960	53
288	16	513	28·5	738	41	970	53·5
297	16·5	522	29	747	41·5	980	54
306	17	531	29·5	756	42	990	54·5
315	17·5	540	30	765	42·5	1000	55
324	18	549	30·5	774	43		

BIBLIOGRAPHY

Roslyn Rensch: THE HARP. G. Duckworth and Co. Ltd., London.

Marcel Tournier: LA HARPE. Henry Lemoine and Co., Editeurs, Paris.

Sergio Paganelli: MUSICAL INSTRUMENTS. Hamlyn, Feltham, Middlesex.

N. B. Challoner: NEW PRECEPTOR FOR THE HARP. (1806). Schott, London.

Carlos Salzedo and L. Lawrence: METHOD FOR THE HARP. G. Schimer, New York.

E. O. Gallagher: IRISH AIRS FOR THE HARP. Walton's Musical Instruments, Dublin.

N. C. Boschsa: METHOD FOR THE HARP. Chappell and Co. Ltd., London.

K. Schlesinger: THE HARP. Encyclopaedia Britannica 1911, London.

D. Diderot and d'Alembert: ENCYCLOPEDIE 1751; Paris.

R. B. Armstrong: THE IRISH AND THE HIGHLAND HARPS. Edinburgh 1904.

G. Bain: CELTIC ART. W. Maclellan, Glasgow.

W. Wheeler and C. H. Hayward: PRACTICAL WOOD CARVING AND GILDING. Evans, London, 1963.

C. M. Lewis and R. H. Warring: GLASS FIBRE FOR AMATEURS. Model and Allied Publications Ltd., Hemel Hempstead.

Supplies for the amateur harp maker are available from the author, G. JAFFRENNOU, Ty-Rhos, St. Monica's Road, Kingsdown, Deal, Kent. Gilding materials are available from G. M. WHILEY Ltd., Victoria Rd., Ruislip, Middx HA4 0LG.